SLOVENIA TRAVEL GUIDE 2025

Discover Hidden Gems, Scenic Wonders, and Cultural Treasures in Europe's Green Heart

ARIA WILD

Copyright © 2024 by Aria Wild

All rights reserved. No part of this publication may be reproduced, distributed, or transmitted in any form or by any means, including photocopying, recording, or other electronic or mechanical methods, without the prior written permission of the publisher, except in the case of brief quotations embodied in critical reviews and certain other noncommercial uses permitted by copyright law. For permission requests, please contact the publisher.

Published by Aria Wild

1600 DOC NICHOLS RD

Durham NC, U.S.A

Cover design by Rodriguez Mitchell

Interior design by Rodriguez Mitchell

Maps by Gabriel Chapman

Editing by Aria Wild

Typesetting by Aria Wild

Photographs by Aria Wild

Printed in U.S.A

TABLE OF CONTENT

INTRODUCTION 5
    WELCOME TO SLOVENIA 5
    WHY VISIT SLOVENIA IN 2025? 9
    HOW TO USE THIS GUIDE 15
CHAPTER ONE 18
    PLANNING YOUR TRIP 18
        BEST TIMES TO VISIT SLOVENIA 18
        VISA AND ENTRY REQUIREMENTS 22
        FLIGHTS AND TRANSPORTATION TO SLOVENIA .26
CHAPTER TWO 31
    GETTING AROUND SLOVENIA 31
        PUBLIC TRANSPORT 31
        DRIVING IN SLOVENIA 36
        CYCLING AND HIKING AS TRANSPORTATION 43
CHAPTER THREE 48
    WHERE TO STAY 48
        BEST CITIES AND REGIONS TO STAY 48
        LUXURY ACCOMMODATIONS AND RESORTS 55
        MID-RANGE HOTELS AND GUESTHOUSES 62
        BUDGET-FRIENDLY HOSTELS AND FARM STAY ..71
CHAPTER FOUR 80
    TOP ATTRACTIONS IN SLOVENIA 80
        LAKE BLED AND BLED CASTLE 80
        LJUBLJANA 84
        PREDLAMA CASTLE AND POSTOJNA CAVE 88
        TRIGLAV NATIONAL PARK 95
CHAPTER FIVE 102
    CULTURAL AND HISTORICAL HIGHLIGHTS 102
        PTUJ 102
        MARIBOR AND THE WORLD'S OLDEST VINE 107
        CULTURAL FESTIVALS AND TRADITIONS 113
        MUSEUMS AND ART GALLERIES 118
CHAPTER SIX 125
    NATURE AND OUTDOOR ACTIVITIES 125
        EXPLORING THE JULIAN ALPS 125
        SOCA VALLEY 131
        CAVES AND KARST LANDSCAPES 136
        SLOVENIAN WINE REGIONS 140
CHAPTER SEVEN 147
    FOOD AND CULINARY EXPERIENCES 147
        TRADITIONAL SLOVENIAN CUISINE 147
        BEST RESTAURANTS ACROSS THE COUNTRY 154
        WINE TASTING IN SLOVENIA'S VINEYARDS 158

LOCAL MARKETS AND FARM-TO-TABLE DINING 162
CHAPTER EIGHT 169
    SHOPPING IN SLOVENIA 169
        UNIQUE ARTISAN CRAFTS AND SOUVENIRS 169
        SHOPPING STREETS IN LJUBLJANA AND BEYOND 174
        LOCAL DELICACIES TO BRING HOME 182
CHAPTER NINE 190
    NIGHTLIFE AND ENTERTAINMENT 190
        BARS AND CAFES IN LJUBLJANA 190
        LIVE MUSIC VENUES AND FESTIVALS 198
        TRADITIONAL FOLK PERFORMANCES 207
CHAPTER TEN 217
    DAY TRIPS AND EXCURSIONS 217
        LAKE BOHINJ 217
        PIRAN AND THE SLOVENIAN COAST 225
        EXPLORING THE KARST REGION 234
        CROSS-BORDER TRIPS TO ITALY, AUSTRIA, OR
        CROATIA 243
CHAPTER ELEVEN 251
    PRACTICAL TIPS FOR TRAVELERS 251
        HEALTH AND SAFETY IN SLOVENIA 251
        BUDGETING AND CURRENCY TIPS 257
        WEATHER AND PACKING ADVICE 264
        ESSENTIAL APPS AND TRAVEL RESOURCES 269
CHAPTER TWELVE.. 277
    SLOVENIA IN 2025 277
        UPCOMING FESTIVALS AND EVENTS 277
        ECO-TOURISM AND SUSTAINABILITY INITIATIVES 284
        HIDDEN GEMS AND EMERGING DESTINATIONS 293
ACKNOWLEGDEMENT 302
        ABOUT THE AUTHOR 302

INTRODUCTION

WELCOME TO SLOVENIA

Welcome to Slovenia, a captivating country where every moment is filled with awe and discovery. Nestled in the heart of Europe, Slovenia offers a unique blend of natural beauty, rich history, and a welcoming atmosphere that invites exploration. Whether you're seeking outdoor adventures, cultural immersion, or moments of relaxation, Slovenia promises an experience like no other.

Begin your journey in Ljubljana, the charming capital city, known for its vibrant riverside cafés, pedestrian-friendly streets, and striking architecture. The city's heart beats in its historical Old Town, where you'll find cobbled streets, Baroque buildings, and the impressive Ljubljana Castle. The Ljubljana River winds through the city, providing the perfect backdrop for leisurely boat rides or scenic walks along the embankments. Don't miss Tivoli Park, a green oasis perfect for a relaxing afternoon, or the bustling Central Market, where you can sample fresh local produce and traditional Slovenian delicacies.

For those with a taste for adventure, Slovenia's landscapes are a playground for outdoor enthusiasts. At Lake Bled, a shimmering jewel surrounded by the towering Julian Alps, you can paddle a traditional pletna boat to the picturesque island or take a hike up to Bled Castle for panoramic views. Just a short distance away,

Lake Bohinj offers serene beauty and a quieter alternative for those looking to escape the crowds. The nearby Triglav National Park is an outdoor paradise, where hiking trails wind through alpine meadows, crystal-clear lakes, and majestic peaks. For the daring, the Soča River offers world-class opportunities for white-water rafting, kayaking, and canyoning in some of the most stunning surroundings in Europe.

Beyond nature, Slovenia is home to historical wonders that reveal its deep cultural roots. Explore the cave systems of Postojna and Škocjan, both UNESCO World Heritage sites, and be awe-struck by the underground world of stalactites, stalagmites, and dramatic rock formations. Predjama Castle, built into the mouth of a cave, stands as one of Europe's most impressive and mysterious fortresses. For a taste of Slovenian history and art, visit the National Gallery and the Museum of Contemporary Art in

Ljubljana, which house impressive collections reflecting the country's rich cultural heritage.

The Slovenian coastline, though small, is a gem that beckons those seeking the charm of the Adriatic. The coastal town of Piran, with its Venetian-inspired architecture and cobbled streets, offers the perfect blend of history and seaside relaxation. The nearby town of Portorož is famous for its beaches and wellness centers, ideal for those looking to unwind in the sun or indulge in rejuvenating spa treatments.

Slovenia's rich culinary scene is another highlight. The country's diverse landscapes contribute to a varied cuisine, where you can savor everything from hearty mountain dishes to fresh seafood from the Adriatic. The wine regions of Goriška Brda, Vipava Valley, and the region around Maribor offer some of the best wines in Europe, with centuries-old traditions and world-class vineyards to explore. Slovenian wine cellars are the perfect places to sample local varieties like the crisp Rebula or the robust Teran, while enjoying the warmth and hospitality of the winemakers.

Whether you're here to hike the Alps, immerse yourself in history, or indulge in culinary delights, Slovenia offers an exceptional variety of experiences. With its mix of breathtaking landscapes, cultural treasures, and unspoiled charm, this small yet remarkable country is ready to captivate your heart and soul. Every corner of Slovenia is an invitation to experience something extraordinary, and there's always more to discover. So take your time, explore the hidden gems, and let Slovenia leave you with memories that will last a lifetime.

WHY VISIT SLOVENIA IN 2025?

Visiting Slovenia in 2025 offers a unique opportunity to explore one of Europe's most dynamic and emerging destinations. The country is constantly evolving, with a growing focus on sustainability, local culture, and a deeper connection to its natural landscapes. Whether you're drawn to Slovenia for its stunning outdoor adventures, rich history, or vibrant culinary scene, 2025 promises to be a year where you can experience all this and more.

Slovenia is renowned for its natural beauty, and in 2025, it continues to offer unparalleled opportunities to connect with the great outdoors. From the emerald waters of Lake Bled to the rugged peaks of the Julian Alps, the country remains a haven for hikers, nature lovers, and adventure seekers. Triglav National Park, the heart of Slovenia's natural wonders, provides extensive trails, crystal-clear rivers, and the iconic Mount Triglav, perfect for those seeking both tranquility and a challenge. The Soča River, famous for its stunning emerald color, offers kayaking, rafting, and other water sports amidst jaw-dropping scenery. Visiting Slovenia in 2025 means experiencing its pristine landscapes in a year that promises more sustainable tourism initiatives, ensuring the protection of its environment for future generations.

Slovenia is also becoming a leader in eco-friendly and sustainable tourism. In 2025, the country continues to emphasize sustainability in both its travel infrastructure and its approach to preserving nature. More eco-conscious accommodations, green-certified restaurants, and environmentally aware travel options are making it easier for visitors to enjoy Slovenia responsibly. Whether you're staying in eco-lodges, cycling through the countryside, or visiting zero-waste markets, Slovenia's commitment to sustainability allows you to enjoy your travels while minimizing your environmental footprint.

Culturally, Slovenia in 2025 will be teeming with new exhibitions, festivals, and events that showcase the country's rich heritage and contemporary creativity. The capital, Ljubljana, continues to be an artistic hub, with galleries, street art, and museums that celebrate Slovenia's history and modern culture. The city will be hosting a variety of festivals, including the Ljubljana Festival, showcasing music, theater, and dance from around the world. Along the coast, Piran's Venetian architecture and the serene atmosphere of the Mediterranean also offer a peaceful and unique way to experience Slovenia's history and culture. Slovenia's festivals, like the Kurentovanje Carnival, promise to deliver even more energy and excitement in 2025, showcasing traditional music, dance, and rituals in colorful celebrations.

Another major reason to visit Slovenia in 2025 is its culinary evolution. Slovenia's cuisine is gaining global recognition, with an increasing number of chefs focusing on local, sustainable, and innovative dishes that reflect the diverse regions of the country. 2025 will see more culinary experiences that highlight Slovenia's rich traditions, including its world-class wine regions such as Goriška Brda and the Vipava Valley. Visitors will have the opportunity to taste authentic dishes prepared with locally sourced ingredients, from delicious pastries to hearty mountain meals, complemented by exquisite wines from Slovenia's centuries-old vineyards.

Slovenia is also home to a fascinating and varied historical and architectural landscape. From the medieval castles like Bled Castle and Predjama Castle to the Baroque and Renaissance buildings in Ljubljana, Slovenia's cultural and historical treasures remain key reasons to visit. The country's commitment to preserving its heritage while embracing modernity ensures that visitors in 2025 will be able to experience both the old and the new in a harmonious and exciting way.

Lastly, Slovenia is simply an undiscovered gem compared to other European destinations. Its compact size means you can explore a diverse range of experiences in a short amount of time, from alpine villages to Mediterranean beaches. With an ever-increasing number of international flights, improving infrastructure, and a reputation for safety and friendliness, Slovenia in 2025 is the perfect year to visit before the crowds of mass tourism arrive.

In essence, 2025 is an exciting time to visit Slovenia because the country is embracing sustainable tourism, celebrating its rich cultural and culinary heritage, and offering exceptional outdoor experiences. Whether you're traveling for relaxation, adventure, or cultural exploration, Slovenia offers the perfect balance of all these elements.

HOW TO USE THIS GUIDE

To use this guide effectively, consider the following steps to make the most of your visit to Slovenia:

Start by familiarizing yourself with the top destinations. This will give you an idea of the most famous spots to visit, like Ljubljana, Lake Bled, and Triglav National Park, and help you decide where to begin your trip. Plan your itinerary based on what interests you the most – whether it's hiking, cultural exploration, or enjoying the coastline.

Next, explore unique experiences mentioned in the guide. Think about what excites you most, whether it's a wine-tasting tour in Goriška Brda, a visit to Postojna Cave, or experiencing a traditional Slovenian festival. These unique experiences will help make your trip memorable and give you a deeper connection to the country.

Consider the best time to visit Slovenia, depending on your interests and the type of weather you'd prefer. Spring and autumn offer mild weather with fewer tourists, while summer is perfect for outdoor activities. Winter is ideal for skiing or enjoying the Christmas markets.

Use the travel tips provided to help you prepare for your trip. This includes practical advice on currency, language, and transportation, ensuring you're well-equipped for your travels. You can also take advantage of suggested itineraries for 3 or 7-day trips if you need help planning your time.

Lastly, keep in mind that Slovenia is an ever-evolving destination, with new sustainable travel options and festivals emerging each year. In 2025, be sure to check out any specific events or eco-tourism initiatives happening, as these will add an extra dimension to your visit.

By following this guide, you'll be able to navigate Slovenia with ease, experience the country's diverse offerings, and create a travel experience that's both enriching and enjoyable.

CHAPTER ONE

PLANNING YOUR TRIP

BEST TIMES TO VISIT SLOVENIA

The best times to visit Slovenia depend on the type of experience you're looking for, as each season offers its own charm. Here's a breakdown of what you can expect during each season:

- Spring (April to June)

Spring is one of the best times to visit Slovenia, as the weather is mild, and nature comes alive with vibrant blooms. This season offers comfortable temperatures, making it ideal for outdoor activities like hiking in the mountains or cycling through the countryside. The crowds are still relatively light, so it's a peaceful time to explore popular destinations such as Lake Bled and Ljubljana. The early summer months of June also mark the start of outdoor festivals and cultural events, adding to the lively atmosphere.

- Summer (July to August)

Summer is peak tourist season in Slovenia, especially in July and August. The weather is warm and sunny, making it perfect for outdoor adventures such as kayaking, rafting, or visiting the country's beautiful lakes and rivers. Slovenia's Adriatic coast becomes a popular spot for those looking to relax by the sea. While this is a great time for those seeking sunshine and vibrant festivals, keep in mind that it can get crowded in major tourist spots. Booking accommodations and tours in advance is recommended during this period.

- Autumn (September to November)

Autumn is another fantastic time to visit Slovenia. The weather is still pleasant in September and October, with fewer tourists than during the summer months. The landscapes transform into a colorful patchwork of reds, oranges, and yellows, making it an ideal time for hiking or enjoying scenic drives, particularly in areas like Triglav National Park and the wine regions. The harvest season also brings fresh local produce, and wine lovers will enjoy attending harvest festivals and wine-tasting tours in regions like Goriška Brda and Maribor. Early autumn offers a perfect balance of good weather and fewer crowds.

- Winter (December to March)

Winter in Slovenia is perfect for those who enjoy snow sports or a cozy, festive atmosphere. The Julian Alps offer excellent skiing and snowboarding opportunities, especially in resorts like Kranjska Gora, Vogel, and Mariborsko Pohorje. If you're looking for a winter wonderland, the country's ski resorts and mountain villages are picturesque and perfect for winter sports enthusiasts. December is also an excellent time for experiencing Slovenia's Christmas markets, especially in Ljubljana, which transforms into a festive, fairy-tale city with twinkling lights and seasonal treats. For those seeking a quieter experience, this is a good time to visit thermal spas or explore the country's historic sites without the crowds.

➢ Best Time for Specific Interests:

1. For outdoor activities like hiking and biking: Spring (April to June) and autumn (September to November) offer the best weather.
2. For wine and food lovers: Late autumn, during the harvest season, is ideal for wine tasting and culinary experiences.
3. For skiing and snow sports: Winter (December to March) is the best time to visit the ski resorts.

Ultimately, the best time to visit Slovenia depends on what you're hoping to experience. Spring and autumn provide the perfect balance of mild weather and fewer crowds, while summer offers vibrant festivals and sunny outdoor activities, and winter is ideal for winter sports and cozy holiday experiences.

VISA AND ENTRY REQUIREMENTS

Slovenia is part of the Schengen Area, so the visa and entry requirements are based on the rules set by the Schengen Agreement. Citizens of the European Union (EU), European Economic Area (EEA) countries, and Switzerland do not need a visa to enter Slovenia. They can travel freely, as long as they have a valid passport or national ID card.

For non-EU citizens, whether you need a visa to enter Slovenia depends on your nationality. Citizens from countries with a visa-free agreement with the Schengen Area can enter Slovenia without a visa for stays up to 90 days within a 180-day period. Some examples of visa-exempt countries include the United States, Canada, Australia, Japan, and New Zealand. If you are from a country that does not have a visa-waiver agreement, you will need to apply for a Schengen visa.

A Schengen visa allows you to stay in Slovenia and other Schengen countries for up to 90 days within a 180-day period for purposes such as tourism, business, or family visits. You will need to apply for this visa before your trip through the Slovenian embassy or consulate in your home country, or through the embassy of another Schengen country if Slovenia is not represented. Common requirements for a Schengen visa include a valid passport (with at least 3 months of validity beyond your planned departure date), a completed visa application form, a passport-sized photo, proof of travel insurance for the Schengen Area, proof of sufficient funds for your stay, and flight and accommodation details. Additional documents may be required depending on the purpose of your visit.

If you arrive in Slovenia from outside the Schengen Area, you will undergo border controls, where your passport and entry requirements will be verified. However, if you're traveling from another Schengen country, there might not be any passport control, as there are no internal border checks within the Schengen Zone.

For short stays of up to 90 days, if you're from a visa-exempt country, you can travel to Slovenia for tourism, business, or family visits without a visa. However, after spending 90 days in any Schengen country, you will need to leave the zone for at least 90 days before returning. It's important to keep track of your travel days to avoid overstaying your permitted time.

If you plan to stay in Slovenia for longer than 90 days for example, for work, study, or family reasons you will need to apply for a long-stay visa or residence permit. The specific requirements depend on the reason for your stay and are typically managed by the Slovenian Ministry of the Interior.

Given the current global health situation, there may be specific health entry requirements, such as proof of vaccination, negative COVID-19 tests, or quarantine, depending on your country of departure. It's essential to check the most up-to-date entry requirements before your trip, as these regulations can change.

It is also advisable to have travel insurance covering medical emergencies, repatriation, and trip cancellations. This is often required for visa applications and provides peace of mind during your travels in Slovenia.

Regarding customs regulations, Slovenia follows standard EU rules. You can bring personal items and goods for personal use, as well as a reasonable amount of alcohol, tobacco, and other products duty-free. Certain items, such as firearms, drugs, and endangered species, are prohibited from being imported into Slovenia.

To ensure a smooth trip, it's important to check with the nearest Slovenian embassy or consulate for the latest information on entry requirements, as these can change frequently due to temporary regulations or unforeseen circumstances.

FLIGHTS AND TRANSPORTATION TO SLOVENIA

Getting to Slovenia is easy thanks to its well-connected transportation network, both for international arrivals and within the country. Here's what you need to know about flights and transportation options to Slovenia.

Slovenia's primary international gateway is Ljubljana Jože Pučnik Airport (LJU), located about 26 kilometers from the capital city. This airport serves several major airlines with direct flights from various European cities, including London, Berlin, Vienna, and Paris. It also offers connections from major hubs in the Middle East and Europe. For travelers coming from outside Europe, connecting flights through larger European airports like Frankfurt, Munich, or Vienna are common.

In addition to Ljubljana's airport, Slovenia's proximity to neighboring countries means that travelers often fly into nearby international airports in Italy, Austria, or Croatia and then travel by road or rail into Slovenia. These airports include Trieste (Italy), Venice (Italy), Zagreb (Croatia), and Klagenfurt (Austria), all of which are within a few hours' drive of Slovenia's borders. From these locations, buses, trains, and rental cars provide easy access to Slovenia.

Once you arrive in Slovenia, you have a variety of transportation options to get around the country. Public transportation is reliable and well-organized, with trains and buses serving most major cities, towns, and tourist attractions. Slovenia's train system is efficient and connects Ljubljana with other cities such as Maribor, Kranj, and Nova Gorica. The bus network is extensive, covering even smaller towns and villages, making it a great way to explore the country.

For a more flexible and personalized experience, renting a car is a popular option for tourists. Slovenia's road infrastructure is excellent, with well-maintained highways and scenic routes that make driving an enjoyable way to explore the countryside and visit more remote locations, like Lake Bohinj or the Karst region. Car rental services are available at the airport, in Ljubljana, and throughout major cities.

If you prefer to travel by taxi or ride-sharing services like Uber, both are available in Ljubljana and other larger cities. These services are convenient for short trips or when public transport options are limited.

For a more scenic and leisurely experience, bicycles are increasingly popular in Slovenia. Many towns offer bike rentals, and the country has a growing network of cycling paths, including routes through vineyards, lakes, and forests. Slovenia is also known for its eco-friendly tourism, so cycling is an environmentally conscious way to explore.

Additionally, boats and ferries can be used to explore Slovenia's small Adriatic coastline. While Slovenia has only a short coastline, Piran and Portorož are popular seaside destinations, and boat trips along the coast are a great way to enjoy the scenic beauty of the region.

Overall, Slovenia offers a range of transportation options to suit every traveler, from convenient public transport to flexible car rentals. Whether you're flying in from another country or exploring the charming towns and beautiful landscapes within Slovenia, getting around is easy and efficient.

CHAPTER TWO

GETTING AROUND SLOVENIA

PUBLIC TRANSPORT

Public transportation in Slovenia is reliable, affordable, and well-connected, making it a convenient option for getting around the country. The system includes trains, buses, and local transport services, all of which offer efficient ways to explore Slovenia's cities, towns, and natural attractions.

- Trains: Slovenia has an extensive and efficient train network operated by Slovenske železnice (Slovenian Railways). The main railway hub is Ljubljana, where most trains depart and arrive. Trains connect Ljubljana to major cities like Maribor, Kranj, Celje, and Nova Gorica, as well as other towns across the country. The train network is also well-connected to neighboring countries, including Austria, Italy, and Croatia. For instance, you can easily take a train from Ljubljana to Venice (Italy) or Zagreb (Croatia). Trains are comfortable, affordable, and offer scenic views of Slovenia's landscapes, especially when traveling through the countryside or near the Alps.

- Buses: Buses are another key form of public transport in Slovenia and serve both urban and rural areas. The Slovenian Bus Company (Avtobusna postaja Ljubljana) operates the main bus station in Ljubljana, with numerous regional and intercity connections. Buses are a great way to reach towns and villages that are not accessible by train, and they also provide connections to Slovenia's tourist attractions like Lake Bled and Postojna Cave. Bus services run regularly, and schedules are available at bus stations or online. While buses in larger cities, such as Ljubljana and Maribor, have frequent schedules, buses between smaller towns might be less frequent.

- Local Public Transport: In Ljubljana, Slovenia's capital, local transportation is organized by Ljubljana Urban Transport (LPP), which operates a fleet of buses that connect various neighborhoods and key areas of the city. Tickets for local buses can be purchased at kiosks, ticket machines, or via the LPP mobile app. Ljubljana also has an efficient bike-sharing system, known as BicikeLJ, which allows visitors and residents to rent bikes for short trips around the city. This is an environmentally friendly and convenient way to explore Ljubljana's sights, such as Tivoli Park, Ljubljana Castle, and the Ljubljanica River.

Other cities, like Maribor, also have local buses, though the service might be less frequent than in Ljubljana. In these cities, buses are often the most affordable way to get around.

- Taxis and Ride-Sharing: While public buses and trains cover most of Slovenia, taxis are also available in larger cities and can be called or flagged down on the street. However, taxis are generally more expensive than buses or trains. Alternatively, ride-sharing services like Uber operate in Ljubljana, making it easy to get around the city and beyond, though availability may vary in smaller towns and rural areas.

- Ferries and Boats: Slovenia has a small Adriatic coastline, and although the transportation network isn't as extensive as in other countries, you can take advantage of boats and ferries to travel along the coast. Ferries run between Piran and nearby locations, and boat trips offer a scenic way to explore Slovenia's coastline and the picturesque town of Piran.

- Tickets and Fare Systems: Tickets for trains and buses can be purchased at stations, online, or via mobile apps. Slovenia uses a contactless payment system for many public transport services, including bus and train rides, where you can use a mobility card or your contactless payment card to board public transport. It's important to check the specific ticket rules and pricing for the service you're using, as fares can vary depending on the route and time of day.

Overall, Slovenia's public transport system is efficient, easy to use, and well-suited for both local travel and exploring the country's main tourist destinations. Whether you're traveling between cities, heading to natural attractions, or simply exploring Ljubljana, public transportation offers a convenient and budget-friendly way to get around.

DRIVING IN SLOVENIA

Driving in Slovenia is relatively straightforward and convenient, as the country has well-maintained roads and highways. Whether you're planning to rent a car or drive your own, here are key things to keep in mind when driving in Slovenia:

- Road Infrastructure: Slovenia has an excellent road network, including modern highways, well-maintained roads, and scenic routes that make driving a pleasant experience. The major highways, especially those connecting cities like Ljubljana, Maribor, and Kranj, are part of the European route system and are generally in good condition. The country is also known for its beautiful, winding roads that pass through its picturesque countryside, including routes to Lake Bled, Triglav National Park, and the coast.

- Driving License: To drive in Slovenia, you must hold a valid driver's license. If you're from an EU or EEA country, your national driving license is sufficient. For non-EU citizens, an International Driving Permit (IDP) is recommended if your license is not in the Latin alphabet. However, you can also drive with a valid driver's license from many countries (including the U.S., Canada, Australia, and others) without an IDP, as long as your license is in English or another widely understood language.

- Road Signs and Traffic Laws: Road signs in Slovenia are standard European signs, with many of them featuring symbols or text in both Slovene and English. It's important to familiarize yourself with the following key traffic laws:

1. Speed Limits: The speed limits are clearly marked and enforced. On highways, the limit is usually 130 km/h (81 mph), while on other main roads, it's typically 90 km/h (56 mph). In urban areas, the limit is usually 50 km/h (31 mph).
2. Alcohol Limit: The legal blood alcohol limit is 0.05%, which is lower than in many other countries. It's safest not to drink at all before driving.
3. Seat Belts: Seat belts are mandatory for all passengers in the car, regardless of where they sit.
4. Mobile Phones: Using a mobile phone while driving without a hands-free device is illegal. Be sure to pull over safely if you need to make a call.
5. Headlights: Headlights must be used throughout the year, even during the day.

This is required by law to improve visibility on Slovenian roads.

- Road Tolls and Vignettes: Slovenia has a toll system for using highways, and vehicles are required to display a vignette (toll sticker) if they plan to drive on motorways and expressways. Vignettes can be purchased for 7 days, one month, or a full year, and they are available at gas stations, border crossings, and online. If you're traveling from nearby countries like Austria, Italy, or Croatia, make sure you buy your vignette before using the highways.

- Parking: Parking in Slovenia is generally straightforward, especially in larger cities like Ljubljana. However, in city centers, parking can be limited and may be subject to time restrictions. Pay attention to parking signs, which will indicate whether parking is free or paid. In Ljubljana, there are designated pay-and-display parking areas, and you may need to buy a ticket from a nearby machine. Parking fines are enforced, so be sure to follow the rules.

- Fuel: Fuel prices in Slovenia are comparable to other European countries. Gas stations are widely available along highways, in towns, and near cities. Most stations accept credit and debit cards, though it's always a good idea to carry some cash for smaller stations in remote areas.

- Driving in Winter: In winter, especially in mountainous regions, conditions can become more challenging. From November to March, it's mandatory to have winter tires on your vehicle if you are traveling in snowy or icy conditions. You may also need to carry chains in some areas, especially when traveling to ski resorts or in more remote regions. Make sure to check weather reports before heading out in winter months.

- Rental Cars: Renting a car in Slovenia is easy, with plenty of rental agencies available at Ljubljana Airport, major cities, and tourist hubs. Rental cars in Slovenia typically come with basic insurance, but you can also opt for additional coverage like collision damage waiver (CDW) or theft protection. Ensure you are aware of the rental terms and fuel policies before renting a car.

- Driving Etiquette: Slovenians generally follow traffic rules carefully. It's essential to drive defensively and be mindful of pedestrians, cyclists, and motorcyclists. When passing through small towns, be aware of speed limits and pedestrians, especially near schools or residential areas. Slovenian drivers are generally respectful, but be prepared for drivers who may be impatient in urban areas.

- Scenic Drives: Slovenia is known for its scenic drives, and a road trip can be an excellent way to explore the country. Some of the most picturesque routes include the drive through the Julian Alps, the Karst region with its caves, and the Slovenian Littoral along the Adriatic coast. Make sure to stop at local viewpoints to enjoy the natural beauty of the country.

In summary, driving in Slovenia is a pleasant experience, with well-maintained roads, clear signage, and a relatively low level of traffic congestion outside the cities. With a valid driving license, knowledge of the road rules, and the appropriate toll vignette, you'll be able to explore Slovenia at your own pace and discover its beautiful landscapes and charming towns.

CYCLING AND HIKING AS TRANSPORTATION

Cycling and hiking are popular and eco-friendly ways to explore Slovenia's stunning landscapes, offering a chance to experience the country's natural beauty up close. Slovenia is well-equipped for both activities, with extensive networks of cycling paths, mountain trails, and well-marked hiking routes, making it a paradise for outdoor enthusiasts.

Cycling in Slovenia is increasingly popular, especially in urban areas. Cities like Ljubljana have a bike-sharing system known as BicikeLJ, making it easy to rent a bike for short trips around the city. With many bike stations located near key attractions, such as Tivoli Park and the Ljubljanica River, cycling is a convenient way to get around and see the sights. Other cities like Maribor and Kranj also offer bike-sharing programs, though on a smaller scale compared to Ljubljana.

For those looking to explore Slovenia's countryside and natural beauty, the country offers a variety of cycling routes, including both mountain biking trails and road cycling routes. The Alpe-Adria Trail, stretching from the Italian Alps to the Adriatic Sea, and the EuroVelo network offer long-distance routes for cyclists. Slovenia's Julian Alps, Lake Bled, and Triglav National Park are some of the most scenic cycling destinations, providing challenging terrain and panoramic views. The country also has a comprehensive network of cycling paths, making it easy to explore from urban areas to remote villages. Bicycle rental services are widely available, and guided bike tours are an excellent option for those wanting to learn more about the region from local experts.

Hiking is another fantastic way to discover Slovenia's diverse landscapes. The Triglav National Park, the country's largest protected area, is home to some of the most iconic hikes, including the challenging Triglav Summit Trail, which leads to Slovenia's highest peak, Mount Triglav. For those seeking less demanding trails, there are numerous shorter hikes around Lake Bled and Lake Bohinj, both offering picturesque paths with views of the surrounding mountains and forests. The Slovenian Mountain Trail is a long-distance hiking route that runs the length of the country, providing hikers with an opportunity to traverse forests, valleys, and alpine meadows. The trail is part of the larger network of European hiking routes in the Alps and is suitable for both novice and experienced hikers.

Slovenia's infrastructure supports both hiking and cycling, with well-marked trails, mountain huts (called koče) located along popular routes for rest and refreshment, and detailed trail maps available for those planning their own adventures. The Slovenian Mountaineering Association (Planinska Zveza Slovenije) provides information and resources for hikers, ensuring that they can navigate the country's diverse terrain safely. Whether you're hiking through the tranquil forests of the lowlands or tackling the higher altitudes of the Julian Alps, Slovenia offers a range of difficulty levels to suit all abilities.

Both hiking and cycling are environmentally friendly forms of travel, and Slovenia promotes these activities as sustainable ways to explore the country. With its commitment to eco-tourism and a growing network of green transportation options, Slovenia encourages visitors to use these methods as alternatives to driving, making it an ideal destination for those looking to enjoy nature while minimizing their environmental impact.

Cycling and hiking tours are available for those who prefer a guided experience. These tours range from leisurely rides through the countryside to more challenging mountain treks. Local guides offer insights into the country's natural history, culture, and traditions, providing a deeper connection to the places you visit. For a more structured experience, several companies specialize in cycling and hiking tours that span several days, allowing you to explore Slovenia in depth.

In conclusion, cycling and hiking are not only recreational activities in Slovenia but also practical ways to explore the country's diverse landscapes. With its excellent infrastructure, commitment to sustainable tourism, and breathtaking scenery, Slovenia is a perfect destination for those who enjoy being active while discovering the beauty of nature. Whether you're biking through alpine meadows or hiking around serene lakes, Slovenia provides endless opportunities for adventure in the great outdoors.

CHAPTER THREE

WHERE TO STAY

BEST CITIES AND REGIONS TO STAY

Slovenia offers a wide variety of cities and regions to stay in, each with its own unique character, atmosphere, and attractions. Whether you're looking for a lively urban experience, a peaceful countryside retreat, or a lakeside escape, Slovenia has something for every type of traveler. Here are some of the best cities and regions to consider staying in when visiting Slovenia.

- Ljubljana

As Slovenia's capital and largest city, Ljubljana is an exciting, vibrant destination. Known for its charming old town, beautiful architecture, and lively atmosphere, it's an excellent base for exploring both the city itself and nearby natural attractions. Must-see landmarks include the Ljubljana Castle, the Triple Bridge, and the Central Market, where you can experience local life and Slovenian cuisine. The city is very walkable and has a strong cycling culture, making it easy to navigate. Ljubljana is also home to a wide range of accommodations, from boutique hotels to modern apartments, and offers plenty of cafes, restaurants, and cultural events. It's also just a short drive from Lake Bled and Lake Bohinj, perfect for day trips.

- Lake Bled

Lake Bled is one of Slovenia's most iconic and beautiful destinations, famous for its emerald-green lake, the charming Bled Island with its picturesque church, and the imposing Bled Castle overlooking the water. Staying in Bled offers an opportunity to enjoy a range of outdoor activities like boating, hiking, and swimming, as well as indulging in the famous Bled cream cake. Accommodations around the lake range from luxury hotels to family-run guesthouses and traditional alpine cottages. The tranquil setting makes Bled a perfect getaway for nature lovers, honeymooners, and anyone looking to relax in one of the most scenic spots in Europe.

- Lake Bohinj

Just a short distance from Lake Bled, Lake Bohinj offers a quieter, less touristy alternative. Nestled in the heart of Triglav National Park, it is a haven for nature lovers and outdoor enthusiasts. Whether you enjoy hiking, kayaking, swimming, or simply soaking in the peaceful surroundings, Lake Bohinj is ideal for those seeking tranquility and natural beauty. The area is also great for winter sports, with nearby Vogel Ski Resort offering skiing and snowboarding. Accommodations in the area include lakeside hotels, cozy mountain lodges, and guesthouses, making it easy to find a place to stay that suits your preferences.

- Maribor

Located in the northeastern part of Slovenia, Maribor is Slovenia's second-largest city and a great base for exploring the Štajerska wine region. The city offers a charming old town, a rich cultural scene, and the famous Lent district along the Drava River. Maribor is known for its historic buildings, vibrant festivals, and for being home to the world's oldest vine, which can be visited in the city center. The surrounding Pohorje Mountains are perfect for skiing in the winter and hiking or cycling in the summer. The city has a variety of accommodations, from luxury hotels to boutique guesthouses, and is an excellent choice for those looking to explore Slovenia's wine culture and beautiful countryside.

- Piran

For a more Mediterranean experience, Piran is Slovenia's most picturesque coastal town. With its Venetian-style architecture, narrow streets, and vibrant harbor, Piran is a charming destination for those seeking a relaxed seaside vacation. The town is known for its medieval old town, with landmarks such as Tartini Square and the St. George's Church, offering stunning views of the Adriatic Sea. The nearby beaches and crystal-clear waters are perfect for swimming, sailing, and sunbathing. Piran is also home to numerous seafood restaurants, where you can enjoy fresh fish and other Mediterranean delicacies. Accommodations in Piran range from boutique hotels to quaint guesthouses, offering a range of options for all budgets.

- Kranjska Gora

Located in the Julian Alps near the borders with Austria and Italy, Kranjska Gora is Slovenia's top destination for outdoor activities year-round. In winter, it's a popular ski resort with slopes suitable for both beginners and more advanced skiers. In summer, Kranjska Gora transforms into a hiking and mountain biking haven, with stunning trails leading into Triglav National Park and the surrounding Alps. The town itself has a charming alpine atmosphere with a variety of hotels, chalets, and guesthouses. Kranjska Gora is perfect for those looking to combine adventure with a cozy mountain retreat.

- The Karst Region

The Karst region in southwestern Slovenia is known for its distinctive landscape of limestone hills, caves, and traditional stone villages. Postojna, the region's largest town, is famous for the Postojna Cave, a vast underground network of caves that can be explored on guided tours. Nearby, Predjama Castle is an incredible medieval fortress built into a cliffside. The Karst region is also renowned for its wine production, particularly Teran wine. Staying in the Karst allows you to enjoy a combination of history, natural beauty, and local culture, with accommodations ranging from cozy rural guesthouses to charming boutique hotels.

- The Soča Valley

The Soča Valley is a breathtakingly beautiful region in western Slovenia, known for the crystal-clear Soča River that runs through it, surrounded by rugged mountains and lush green landscapes. The valley is a popular destination for outdoor activities such as kayaking, rafting, hiking, and cycling, as well as for visiting World War I sites. The town of Bovec is the main hub in the valley, offering a range of accommodations from rustic guesthouses to luxurious hotels. The Soča Valley is ideal for those who love adventure and nature and want to explore Slovenia's history and natural wonders.

In conclusion, Slovenia offers a diverse range of cities and regions to suit all types of travelers. From the vibrant capital of Ljubljana to the tranquil lakes of Bled and Bohinj, the charming coastal town of Piran, and the adventure-filled Soča Valley, Slovenia has something to offer everyone. Whether you're seeking a cultural city break, an outdoor adventure, or a relaxing getaway, Slovenia's cities and regions provide the perfect setting for a memorable trip.

LUXURY ACCOMMODATIONS AND RESORTS

Slovenia offers a range of luxury accommodations and resorts that combine world-class service, stunning natural surroundings, and exceptional amenities. Whether you're looking for a lavish spa experience, a mountain retreat, or a lakeside escape, Slovenia has several top-tier options to make your stay unforgettable.

- Grand Hotel Toplice (Lake Bled)

One of the most iconic luxury hotels in Slovenia, Grand Hotel Toplice is located right on the shores of Lake Bled. This historic hotel offers a blend of elegance and traditional alpine charm, with rooms featuring stunning lake views and classic interiors. Guests can enjoy an exclusive spa, private beach access, and fine dining in the hotel's restaurant overlooking the lake. The hotel also has a luxury wellness center, offering a range of treatments designed for relaxation and rejuvenation. Its proximity to Bled Castle and Bled Island makes it an ideal base for exploring the region while enjoying luxurious amenities.

- InterContinental Ljubljana (Ljubljana)

For those seeking luxury in Slovenia's capital, the InterContinental Ljubljana offers a modern and sophisticated experience. Located in the city center, this 5-star hotel boasts spacious rooms with panoramic views of Ljubljana, top-tier dining options, and an extensive wellness area. The hotel's Sky Lounge offers cocktails and an unbeatable view of the city and the nearby Alps. Guests can also enjoy the hotel's spa facilities, including a sauna, hot tub, and a fully equipped fitness center. The InterContinental is perfect for travelers who want to experience Ljubljana's vibrant atmosphere while staying in a luxury environment.

- Hotel Belvedere (Lake Bled)

Another luxurious lakeside option in Lake Bled is the Hotel Belvedere. This 4-star hotel is perched on a hill, offering breathtaking views of the lake, the surrounding mountains, and Bled Island. Known for its serene atmosphere and excellent service, Hotel Belvedere is an excellent choice for guests seeking relaxation and luxury. The hotel offers upscale rooms, a wellness center with a sauna, and a restaurant with an emphasis on local cuisine. The outdoor pool provides a perfect spot to unwind, with a panoramic backdrop of Lake Bled.

- Kempinski Palace Portorož (Portorož)

Located along Slovenia's Adriatic coast, Kempinski Palace Portorož is one of the country's most luxurious resorts. The hotel is set in a beautifully restored historic building, combining classic elegance with modern comfort. Guests can enjoy world-class spa facilities, a private beach, fine dining, and beautiful sea views. The hotel's Palace Spa offers a range of treatments, including facials, massages, and wellness therapies. For those seeking a romantic getaway or a relaxing seaside holiday, Kempinski is the ultimate luxury destination.

- Thermana Park Laško (Laško)

For those seeking a more wellness-focused experience, Thermana Park Laško is an outstanding luxury resort. Set in the picturesque Laško region, the resort offers a large thermal spa complex with hot spring pools, saunas, and a wide range of wellness treatments. The 5-star hotel features modern, comfortable rooms, many of which have balconies with views of the surrounding nature. Guests can indulge in high-end spa therapies, enjoy gourmet dining, or explore the peaceful countryside. Thermana Park

Laško is perfect for those looking to relax, rejuvenate, and enjoy Slovenia's thermal waters.

- Adora Hotel (Ljubljana)

For those who appreciate modern elegance with a boutique feel, Adora Hotel in Ljubljana offers an intimate yet luxurious experience. Located near the historic city center, this 4-star hotel combines stylish design with personalized service. Guests can enjoy spacious, contemporary rooms with high-end amenities, an on-site restaurant, and easy access to Ljubljana's cultural landmarks, including Ljubljana Castle and Tivoli Park. Adora Hotel is ideal for travelers looking for a quieter, more exclusive stay while being close to the vibrant energy of the capital city.

- Dvor Jezeršek (Zgornja Besnica)

For a unique luxury experience that focuses on authentic Slovenian culture and cuisine, Dvor Jezeršek offers a charming setting. Located just outside Ljubljana, in Zgornja Besnica, this boutique hotel is set within a traditional Slovenian manor. Guests can enjoy a personalized stay with locally sourced food and wine, luxury accommodations, and a range of bespoke experiences, such as private cooking classes and wine tastings. Its serene setting and focus on local heritage make it a great option for those looking to explore Slovenian culture in a luxurious yet intimate environment.

- Rikli Balance Hotel (Lake Bled)

The Rikli Balance Hotel, part of the Sava Hotels & Resorts chain, is another excellent luxury option in Lake Bled. This 4-star hotel offers panoramic views of the lake and the Julian Alps, combined with a focus on wellness and relaxation. The hotel's spa and wellness center features a sauna, massage rooms, and an outdoor pool overlooking the lake. Guests can enjoy healthy cuisine in the hotel's restaurant and explore the surrounding nature with hiking, biking, or boat rides on Lake Bled.

- Hotel Alpine (Kranjska Gora)

For a luxurious stay in the Slovenian Alps, Hotel Alpine in Kranjska Gora offers a combination of Alpine charm and modern amenities. This 4-star resort caters to both winter sports enthusiasts and those seeking a peaceful getaway in the mountains. The hotel provides easy access to skiing and snowboarding in winter, while the summer months offer hiking and cycling opportunities. The hotel has an exclusive wellness center, featuring a sauna, hot tub, and a selection of treatments designed for relaxation after a day of outdoor activities.

- LIPA Resort (Slovenian Countryside)

LIPA Resort, located in the tranquil countryside of Slovenia, is a luxury resort offering an immersive nature experience with luxurious amenities. The resort combines sleek modern architecture with eco-friendly principles, offering spacious villas, an upscale spa, and gourmet dining focused on organic, locally sourced ingredients. For those looking to unwind and escape the hustle and bustle, LIPA Resort offers a peaceful and serene environment for relaxation, wellness, and outdoor adventures.

Slovenia's luxury accommodations and resorts combine exceptional service, natural beauty, and unique experiences to offer guests a truly memorable stay. Whether you're seeking relaxation, adventure, wellness, or cultural exploration, these high-end options cater to a range of preferences, ensuring that your time in Slovenia is both luxurious and unforgettable.

MID-RANGE HOTELS AND GUESTHOUSES

Slovenia offers a variety of mid-range hotels and guesthouses that provide a comfortable stay without breaking the bank. These accommodations offer great value, combining quality service, convenient locations, and cozy atmospheres, perfect for those who want a balance of comfort and affordability. Here are some of the best mid-range options in Slovenia:

- Hotel Park (Lake Bled)

Hotel Park is one of the best mid-range hotels in Lake Bled, offering a great combination of comfort, location, and affordability. Situated right on the lakeshore, the hotel offers beautiful views of Lake Bled and is within walking distance of the Bled Castle and the famous Bled Island. The hotel features modern rooms with contemporary amenities, and guests can enjoy a wellness area with saunas and a fitness center. The on-site restaurant serves a variety of Slovenian and international dishes, and the hotel is a great base for exploring Bled and the surrounding area.

- City Hotel (Ljubljana)

Located in the heart of Ljubljana, City Hotel offers an ideal location for those who want to explore the capital's historic center, shops, and restaurants. The hotel offers comfortable, modern rooms with a focus on practicality and comfort. Guests can enjoy a delicious breakfast buffet, and the hotel's central location makes it easy to explore the city on foot, including nearby attractions like the Ljubljana Castle, Triple Bridge, and Central Market. The City Hotel offers a great value for travelers who want to stay in the center of Ljubljana without spending a fortune.

- Hotel Kovač (Kranjska Gora)

Nestled in the charming alpine town of Kranjska Gora, Hotel Kovač offers a cozy and affordable option for those visiting this popular ski resort. The hotel is situated near the town center and offers easy access to ski slopes, hiking trails, and the Triglav National Park. Rooms are simple yet comfortable, and the hotel features a sauna, ski storage facilities, and a restaurant that serves traditional Slovenian dishes. Hotel Kovač is a great mid-range option for winter sports enthusiasts or those looking to enjoy the stunning alpine scenery.

- Hotel Piran (Piran)

In the charming coastal town of Piran, Hotel Piran offers comfortable accommodations with beautiful views of the Adriatic Sea. This hotel is within walking distance of the town's main attractions, including the Tartini Square, St. George's Church, and the seaside promenade. The hotel has a rooftop terrace with a bar and views of the coastline, making it a great place to unwind after a day of exploring. The rooms are modern and well-equipped, and the hotel's location allows guests to experience the Mediterranean charm of Piran without the high prices of luxury resorts.

- Hotel Bohinj (Lake Bohinj)

Located in Lake Bohinj, Hotel Bohinj is a mid-range hotel offering a peaceful and comfortable stay in one of Slovenia's most beautiful natural settings. The hotel is surrounded by the Triglav National Park and offers easy access to hiking, swimming, and other outdoor activities. Rooms are modern, with wooden accents that complement the natural surroundings, and the hotel features a wellness center with a sauna and hot tub. The on-site restaurant serves local cuisine, and the hotel is an excellent choice for visitors seeking relaxation and nature in a tranquil setting.

- Hotel Maribor (Maribor)

Located in Maribor, Slovenia's second-largest city, Hotel Maribor offers a modern and stylish stay with easy access to the city's historic center and nearby attractions, including the famous Old Vine House and the Lent district. The hotel offers a variety of room types, ranging from standard to more spacious suites, all featuring contemporary décor and amenities. Guests can enjoy a well-equipped wellness center, an on-site restaurant, and a wine bar serving local wines from the surrounding Štajerska wine region. Hotel Maribor is a great option for travelers who want to experience the culture, history, and gastronomy of the area.

- Guesthouse Zupančič (Lake Bled)

For a more intimate and personal experience, Guesthouse Zupančič in Lake Bled offers comfortable rooms in a peaceful, family-run guesthouse setting. The guesthouse is just a short walk from Lake Bled and offers easy access to Bled's main attractions. Rooms are cozy, and the property offers a lovely garden, making it a great spot for a relaxing stay. The guesthouse's restaurant serves traditional Slovenian dishes, and the owners are known for their warm hospitality. This is an ideal choice for visitors seeking a homier, more affordable option near Lake Bled.

- Hotel Sunrose 7 (Portorož)

Located in Portorož, a coastal town on the Slovenian Adriatic, Hotel Sunrose 7 is a stylish mid-range hotel that offers a mix of modern design and comfort. The hotel features spacious rooms with contemporary furnishings, a wellness center with a sauna, and an outdoor pool. Guests can also enjoy dining at the hotel's Mediterranean-inspired restaurant, which focuses on fresh, local ingredients. With easy access to the beach and the town's popular promenade, this hotel is an excellent option for those looking to enjoy the coastal charm of Portorož without the high prices of luxury resorts.

- Guesthouse Triglav (Bohinj)

For a more rustic experience in the Lake Bohinj area, Guesthouse Triglav offers a cozy, family-run atmosphere in a quiet part of the Triglav National Park. The guesthouse features traditional alpine decor and comfortable rooms with stunning views of the surrounding mountains. Guests can enjoy a hearty breakfast in the morning and dine on homemade Slovenian dishes in the evening. The location makes it ideal for those looking to explore Lake Bohinj, hike in the Julian Alps, or simply relax in nature.

- Hotel Cerkno (Cerkno)

Located in the Cerkno region, Hotel Cerkno offers a modern and comfortable stay with easy access to outdoor activities in both summer and winter. The hotel is close to the Cerkno Ski Resort, making it a popular choice for winter sports enthusiasts, but it also offers hiking and mountain biking opportunities in the warmer months. The hotel features comfortable rooms, a wellness center with a sauna and hot tub, and an on-site restaurant serving local Slovenian dishes. Hotel Cerkno provides great value for those seeking both relaxation and adventure.

- Hotel Zeleni Gaj (Šmarješke Toplice)

For a wellness-focused stay, Hotel Zeleni Gaj in the Šmarješke Toplice region offers comfortable accommodations alongside access to Slovenia's famous thermal spas. The hotel is set in a peaceful, rural location with easy access to hiking and biking trails. It's ideal for those seeking relaxation in a quiet setting with high-quality wellness facilities, including thermal pools, saunas, and spa treatments. Guests can enjoy healthy, locally sourced meals in the hotel's restaurant. This hotel is perfect for travelers looking to combine comfort with relaxation in a natural environment.

In conclusion, Slovenia's mid-range hotels and guesthouses offer a variety of accommodation options that strike a balance between comfort, affordability, and great service. Whether you prefer lakeside views, coastal escapes, or mountain retreats, you'll find plenty of welcoming options across the country to suit your travel needs.

BUDGET-FRIENDLY HOSTELS AND FARM STAY

Slovenia is home to several budget-friendly hostels and farm stays that provide affordable, comfortable accommodations while allowing travelers to experience the country's natural beauty and authentic local culture. Whether you are a backpacker, a solo traveler, or a group of friends, these options offer great value for money without compromising on comfort or location.

Hostels in Slovenia

- Hostel Celica (Ljubljana)

One of the most unique hostels in Slovenia, Hostel Celica is housed in a former prison, offering guests a quirky, artistic stay. Located in Ljubljana, this hostel is a short walk from the city's main attractions, including Ljubljana Castle and the Triple Bridge. Each room is individually designed by different artists, giving the hostel a creative and vibrant atmosphere. The hostel offers both dormitory-style rooms and private rooms, making it a great option for both budget-conscious solo travelers and groups. The hostel also has a café and bar, and guests can enjoy the communal spaces, making it a social hub for travelers.

- Vila Veselova (Ljubljana)

Vila Veselova is a charming, budget-friendly hostel located in the heart of Ljubljana. Set in a beautiful villa surrounded by a peaceful garden, it offers a cozy and relaxing environment for travelers. The hostel offers both dormitory and private rooms at affordable prices. It's a great choice for those seeking a quiet stay in a central location, with easy access to the city's historical landmarks, parks, and riverside areas. Vila Veselova is also known for its welcoming atmosphere and communal spaces, ideal for meeting fellow travelers.

- Hostel Tresor (Ljubljana)

Situated in the center of Ljubljana, Hostel Tresor is an excellent choice for budget-conscious travelers. Housed in a historic building that was once a bank, this hostel combines a central location with modern amenities. The hostel offers a variety of room options, from dorms to private rooms, all designed with comfort in mind. Hostel Tresor features a trendy bar and a lounge area where guests can relax and socialize. It's just a short walk from the Ljubljana Castle, the Central Market, and many other popular sites, making it a great base for exploring the city.

- H2O Hostel (Bled)

For those looking to stay near Lake Bled, H2O Hostel offers a budget-friendly option with a great location just a short walk from the lake. This lively, modern hostel offers dormitory and private rooms, all with contemporary decor. H2O Hostel features a communal kitchen, bar, and a cozy common room where guests can unwind. Its proximity to the lake means you can easily enjoy outdoor activities like swimming, boating, and hiking. The hostel also organizes various social events and tours, making it a great place to meet fellow travelers.

- Tina Hostel (Piran)

Located in the picturesque coastal town of Piran, Tina Hostel offers a budget-friendly stay with easy access to the beach and the town's historical sites. The hostel has a laid-back, relaxed atmosphere and offers both dorms and private rooms, perfect for travelers looking to enjoy Piran without spending too much. The town's stunning Tartini Square and St. George's Church are just a short walk away. Tina Hostel is a great base for exploring the beautiful Slovenian coast while enjoying affordable accommodations.

Farm Stays in Slovenia

- Farm Stay Na Škofji (Pivka)

Located in the serene countryside near Pivka, Farm Stay Na Škofji offers guests a chance to experience authentic Slovenian rural life. This family-run farm stay allows guests to stay in comfortable rooms with rustic décor, while enjoying the natural beauty of the surrounding landscape. Guests can participate in farm activities such as milking cows, picking fruit, or helping with vegetable harvesting. The hosts also offer homemade meals prepared with fresh, locally grown ingredients, making this farm stay a true culinary experience. It's a peaceful and budget-friendly option for those wanting to get away from the hustle and bustle of city life.

- Kmetija Pugelj (Ljubljana)

Just a short distance from Ljubljana, Kmetija Pugelj is a charming farm stay that offers both accommodation and an authentic Slovenian farm experience. The property is surrounded by beautiful landscapes, including forests, fields, and vineyards. Guests can enjoy fresh, homemade products like jams, cheeses, and cured meats. The hosts offer a variety of farm activities, from helping with animal care to learning about traditional farming practices. The family-friendly environment and tranquil surroundings make it a great choice for those looking for a rural escape while still being close to the capital.

- Farm Stay Pri Martinovih (Radovljica)

Located in the picturesque Radovljica region, Farm Stay Pri Martinovih is an excellent option for those looking to immerse themselves in nature while enjoying affordable accommodation. Set among rolling hills and close to Lake Bled, this family-operated farm offers cozy rooms with beautiful views of the surrounding countryside. Guests can enjoy homemade meals made with fresh ingredients from the farm, as well as participate in farm activities, including milking cows and feeding animals. The farm is also a great base for hiking and exploring nearby attractions, including Triglav National Park.

- Turistična Kmetija Zorko (Velenje)

Located in the Velenje region, Turistična Kmetija Zorko offers a peaceful farm stay experience. The property is set in a quiet rural area, surrounded by fields and forests. The farm offers traditional Slovenian hospitality, with homemade food prepared from local produce. Guests can enjoy the peaceful countryside, go hiking, or explore nearby attractions, such as Velenje Castle or Lake Velenje. This farm stay is perfect for those seeking a quiet retreat with a chance to experience life on a working Slovenian farm.

- Farm Stay Janko (Bohinj)

For those visiting the beautiful Lake Bohinj area, Farm Stay Janko offers an authentic and budget-friendly stay. Situated in the heart of the Julian Alps, this farm stay is ideal for nature lovers and outdoor enthusiasts. The rooms are simple yet comfortable, with views of the surrounding mountains and forests. Guests can enjoy traditional homemade meals and experience daily life on the farm, including helping with animals and harvesting produce. The location is perfect for those looking to explore the stunning natural beauty of Triglav National Park, with hiking and cycling opportunities just a short distance away.

- Farm Stay Zajc (Mojstrana)

Located near the charming village of Mojstrana, Farm Stay Zajc offers an affordable and authentic experience of Slovenian rural life. The farm is nestled in the mountains, offering peaceful surroundings and breathtaking views. Guests can enjoy homemade meals, with fresh ingredients sourced from the farm itself. The hosts also offer guided tours of the farm, allowing visitors to learn about the various agricultural activities taking place. This farm stay is a great option for those looking to experience the tranquility of Slovenia's countryside while being close to hiking trails and Triglav National Park.

Slovenia's budget-friendly hostels and farm stays provide an excellent way to experience the country's diverse landscapes and authentic local culture while keeping costs low. Whether you are exploring Ljubljana, the Slovenian coast, or the Alpine regions, these affordable accommodations offer great value for money, along with unique experiences that you won't find in traditional hotels. From quirky urban hostels to peaceful rural farm stays, Slovenia has plenty of options for travelers on a budget.

CHAPTER FOUR

TOP ATTRACTIONS IN SLOVENIA

LAKE BLED AND BLED CASTLE

Lake Bled is one of Slovenia's most iconic and picturesque destinations, offering stunning views and a wealth of outdoor activities. Nestled in the Julian Alps, the lake is a glacial body of water known for its crystal-clear emerald waters, which provide a stunning contrast to the surrounding green forests and snow-capped mountains. The centerpiece of Lake Bled is Bled Island, a small island located in the middle of the lake, home to the Church of the Assumption. The island is accessible by traditional pletna boats, which are rowed by local boatmen dressed in traditional attire. The boat ride to the island is an essential experience for visitors, and once on the island, visitors can ring the wishing bell in the church, a popular tradition believed to grant good luck.

Lake Bled is surrounded by a scenic walking and cycling path, perfect for leisurely strolls or bike rides while taking in the breathtaking views. The lake is an excellent spot for swimming during the warmer months, and kayaking is another popular activity for those looking to explore the water in a more adventurous way. Additionally, Vintgar Gorge, located just a short distance away, offers a picturesque hike through a narrow gorge with wooden boardwalks above the river, providing an unforgettable experience for nature lovers.

Another highlight of Lake Bled is Bled Castle, perched high above the lake on a cliff that offers panoramic views of the surrounding area. Bled Castle is one of Slovenia's oldest castles, dating back over 1,000 years. The castle's complex includes several buildings, including a chapel, a museum detailing the history of the castle and the surrounding region, a wine cellar, and a printing press where visitors can learn about medieval printing techniques. The courtyard of the castle is a beautiful spot to relax, take in the views, and explore the historical exhibits. The castle also offers wine tastings, where guests can sample local wines while enjoying the stunning vistas of the lake.

Overall, Lake Bled and Bled Castle are essential destinations for any traveler visiting Slovenia. Whether you're enjoying a peaceful boat ride, exploring the historical castle, hiking the surrounding trails, or simply relaxing by the lake, these attractions offer an unforgettable experience filled with natural beauty and cultural heritage.

LJUBLJANA

Ljubljana, the capital of Slovenia, is a charming and vibrant city that seamlessly blends historical heritage with modern-day culture. Known for its picturesque old town, green spaces, and eco-friendly initiatives, Ljubljana offers a welcoming atmosphere for visitors looking to experience both the culture and natural beauty of Slovenia.

The heart of the city is the Ljubljanica River, which flows through the center, flanked by narrow streets, colorful buildings, and lively cafés. The river is crossed by several beautiful bridges, the most iconic being the Triple Bridge, designed by the renowned architect Jože Plečnik. The city is very walkable, with pedestrian zones and bridges that connect the old town to newer areas. The combination of historic landmarks and modern infrastructure makes Ljubljana one of Europe's most livable and attractive capitals.

A highlight of Ljubljana is the Ljubljana Castle, perched on a hill overlooking the city. Dating back to the 11th century, the castle offers fantastic views of the city and surrounding countryside. Visitors can take a funicular to the top or hike up the hill to explore the castle's museum, exhibition spaces, and chapel. The castle also hosts cultural events, concerts, and a popular café with panoramic views.

Preseren Square, named after Slovenia's national poet France Prešeren, is the central gathering place in Ljubljana. The square is surrounded by elegant architecture and is home to a statue of Prešeren, as well as the Franciscan Church of the Annunciation, a beautiful Baroque-style church that adds to the charm of the square. This area is a hub for social life, with outdoor cafés and street performances throughout the year.

Ljubljana is also known for its vibrant art scene and cultural events, such as the annual Ljubljana

Festival, which showcases classical music, ballet, and opera performances. The National Gallery of Slovenia and the Museum of Modern Art offer a deep dive into Slovenian art and history. The city's commitment to sustainability is evident in its numerous green spaces, such as Tivoli Park, which is perfect for a relaxing stroll or a picnic, and Rožnik Hill, where you can enjoy nature and spectacular views of the city.

Food lovers will find plenty to enjoy in Ljubljana, with an array of restaurants, cafés, and markets offering local Slovenian dishes as well as international cuisine. The Central Market, located near the river, is a great place to sample fresh produce, local cheeses, meats, and traditional treats. Ljubljana is also home to several innovative and eco-conscious eateries, reflecting the city's commitment to sustainability.

Metelkova City, an autonomous cultural center located in the heart of Ljubljana, offers an alternative side to the city. Originally a military barracks, it has been transformed into a lively space filled with galleries, music venues, bars, and street art. This area is perfect for those interested in Ljubljana's counterculture and artistic expression.

Ljubljana is also very well connected, making it an ideal base for exploring Slovenia's diverse landscapes. It's easy to take day trips from the city to Lake Bled, Postojna Cave, Triglav National Park, or the Slovenian coast. The city's efficient public transport system, including buses and bikes, allows visitors to easily get around and enjoy all that Ljubljana has to offer.

Overall, Ljubljana is a city that effortlessly combines history, culture, nature, and modernity. Its intimate size, vibrant atmosphere, and focus on sustainability make it a wonderful destination for travelers looking to experience the best of Slovenia. Whether you're strolling along the river, exploring its historic sites, or enjoying its lively cultural scene, Ljubljana has something for everyone.

PREDLAMA CASTLE AND POSTOJNA CAVE

Predjama Castle and Postojna Cave are two of Slovenia's most captivating natural and historical attractions, offering a unique blend of stunning landscapes, medieval architecture, and underground wonders. Both are located in the Karst region of Slovenia, making them perfect companions for a day trip or excursion from Ljubljana.

- Predjama Castle

Predjama Castle (Predjamski grad) is a striking medieval fortress built into the mouth of a cave, perched high above the Lokva River in the Karst region. The castle is one of Slovenia's most famous landmarks due to its unique location and dramatic setting. It dates back to the 12th century, although much of its current structure was added in the 16th century. The castle is built into the side of a 100-meter-high cliff, blending seamlessly with the surrounding rock formations and cave openings. Its strategic position made it nearly impregnable in medieval times, and it was a symbol of power for the local nobility.

The castle is famous for its connection to the legend of Erazem of Predjama, a knight robber who resisted the Habsburg empire in the 15th century. According to legend, Erazem used a hidden passageway in the castle to escape during a siege and to bring food and supplies. Today, visitors can tour the castle's interiors, which include historical exhibitions, armor displays, and furnishings that recreate medieval life. The castle also offers a chance to explore its cave system, which includes hidden tunnels and chambers, further adding to the intrigue and allure of this fascinating site.

The Predjama Castle Museum provides insights into the history of the castle, its medieval defense mechanisms, and the legend of Erazem. Visitors can also enjoy panoramic views of the surrounding countryside, including the Lokva River, which winds its way through the valley below.

- Postojna Cave

Just a short drive from Predjama Castle, the Postojna Cave (Postojnska jama) is one of Slovenia's most popular natural attractions. This 16-kilometer-long cave system is one of the largest and most impressive of its kind in Europe. It is famous for its vast stalactite and stalagmite formations, underground passages, and breathtaking chambers, some of which are so large they could house an entire cathedral. The cave is one of the most visited tourist attractions in Slovenia and offers a fascinating glimpse into the natural history of the region.

A visit to Postojna Cave typically begins with a guided train ride that takes visitors deep into the cave system. The ride covers several kilometers of the cave, offering views of the impressive formations. Once inside the cave, visitors can disembark to explore on foot, taking in highlights such as the Great Hall, the Tunnel of the Fairy Tale, and the Concert Hall, where the acoustics are so perfect that concerts have been held there. The Postojna Cave is a living cave, meaning that the formations are still growing, and visitors can witness the ongoing process of geological change.

One of the most unique aspects of Postojna Cave is its population of olms, also known as human fish (Proteus anguinus), which are rare aquatic salamanders that live in the cave's dark, underwater chambers. These blind creatures have adapted to the cave's subterranean environment, and they are often a point of interest for visitors.

In addition to exploring the cave, visitors can also visit the Postojna Cave Park, which includes the Postojna Cave Visitor Center, where you can learn about the cave's history, geology, and the efforts made to preserve the cave system. The park also includes the Vivarium, a research facility that houses a variety of local and exotic species, including the famous olms, and offers educational exhibits.

➢ Visiting Tips

Both Predjama Castle and Postojna Cave can be visited on the same day, as they are located just a short distance apart. For a full experience, it's recommended to start with Predjama Castle in the morning, exploring its fascinating history and dramatic architecture, before heading to Postojna Cave in the afternoon to marvel at the underground world.

➤ How to Get There

Both attractions are easily accessible by car from Ljubljana, and there are also organized tours available for visitors who prefer guided trips. Public transport options, including buses, are available, but may require some transfers.

Predjama Castle and Postojna Cave are two of Slovenia's most stunning and historically significant attractions, offering visitors a unique opportunity to experience both the natural beauty and medieval history of the region. Whether exploring the medieval fortress built into the cave's mouth or venturing deep underground to discover the marvels of Postojna Cave, these sites provide a memorable experience that showcases the best of Slovenia's Karst landscape and rich cultural heritage.

TRIGLAV NATIONAL PARK

Triglav National Park is Slovenia's only national park, located in the Julian Alps in the northwestern part of the country. It covers an area of approximately 838 square kilometers, making it a haven for outdoor enthusiasts and nature lovers. The park is named after Triglav, Slovenia's highest peak, which stands at 2,864 meters, and serves as a symbol of the country. Triglav National Park is renowned for its breathtaking landscapes, diverse wildlife, and rich natural heritage. It offers some of the most spectacular mountain landscapes in Europe, with towering peaks, glacial lakes, cascading waterfalls, deep ravines, and lush valleys.

One of the most iconic features of the park is Triglav Mountain, the centerpiece of the park and the highest peak in Slovenia. The mountain holds a special place in Slovenian culture, and climbing it is a popular challenge for hikers and mountaineers. The ascent to the summit is demanding, requiring preparation and an experienced guide, but it rewards climbers with panoramic views of the surrounding mountains and valleys. For those who prefer a less strenuous experience, there are Triglav huts located at lower altitudes where visitors can enjoy the beauty of the region without having to climb the mountain itself.

The Soča River, which flows through the valley, is another prominent feature of the park. Known for its striking turquoise-blue waters, the river is a paradise for water sports enthusiasts. Activities like white-water rafting, kayaking, and canyoning are popular in the Soča Valley, and the river's beauty is unmatched. The valley is also historically significant, with several World War I sites scattered throughout the region, offering a glimpse into the past amid the stunning natural scenery.

Lake Bohinj, Slovenia's largest lake, is located within the boundaries of the park. Surrounded by the mountains of the Julian Alps, the lake offers a peaceful setting for swimming, kayaking, and hiking. In the winter, the nearby Vogel Ski Resort becomes a hub for skiing and snowboarding, turning the area into a year-round destination. Savica Waterfall, located near Lake Bohinj, is one of the park's most famous natural landmarks, with its impressive 78-meter drop attracting visitors year-round.

Triglav National Park is also home to several waterfalls and gorges, such as the Peričnik Waterfall and Vintgar Gorge. Peričnik is a two-tiered waterfall that allows visitors to walk behind it, offering unique views. Vintgar Gorge is a popular hiking destination, where visitors can walk along wooden boardwalks that lead through the narrow gorge, offering views of the crystal-clear water and surrounding nature.

In terms of wildlife, Triglav National Park is a treasure trove of biodiversity. The park is home to rare species such as the golden eagle, chamois, red deer, and the elusive lynx. It is also home to a variety of wildflowers, particularly in the spring and summer, when alpine meadows come alive with color. The park's diversity of ecosystems makes it a haven for nature lovers, birdwatchers, and botanists.

The park offers an extensive network of hiking trails, with options for all levels of hikers. Whether you're looking for a leisurely walk by the river or a challenging alpine hike, Triglav National Park has something for everyone. One of the most popular treks is the Seven Lakes Valley, which leads hikers through lush valleys and past stunning glacial lakes, offering a truly memorable experience. For those looking for a more challenging adventure, multi-day hikes like the Triglav Lakes Valley trek take visitors through remote areas of the park, past mountain huts, and offer stunning views of the surrounding peaks.

Triglav National Park is also a fantastic destination for cycling. The Soča Valley offers scenic routes that are suitable for both road cyclists and mountain bikers. The park's trails wind through picturesque villages, past rivers, and offer incredible mountain vistas, making it an ideal destination for cycling enthusiasts.

During the winter months, the park transforms into a winter sports haven. Areas around Lake Bohinj and Vogel Ski Resort are popular for skiing, snowboarding, and snowshoeing. The snow-covered peaks of the Julian Alps offer perfect conditions for winter activities, and the park becomes a serene winter landscape.

Wildlife watching is another popular activity in Triglav National Park. Visitors can spot golden eagles, griffon vultures, and lammergeiers soaring above the mountains, and with a bit of luck, encounter mammals such as chamois or red deer. The park's diverse habitats offer ample opportunities for wildlife enthusiasts to explore and discover the rich fauna that inhabits the region.

Triglav National Park is easily accessible from Ljubljana, Slovenia's capital, which is about a 1.5-hour drive away. It is also close to the popular Lake Bled region, making it an excellent day trip for visitors to the area. The park is well-served by a network of roads, and visitors can also explore the area on foot, by bike, or with organized tours.

Triglav National Park offers a pristine, protected space where visitors can enjoy the best of Slovenia's natural beauty, from the towering peaks and glaciers of the Julian Alps to the lush valleys and sparkling lakes below. With its diverse ecosystems, vast network of hiking trails, and numerous outdoor activities, Triglav National Park is a must-visit destination for anyone seeking adventure, peace, or a deeper connection with nature. Whether you're hiking to the summit of Triglav, rafting along the Soča River, or simply enjoying the beauty of the alpine lakes and meadows, Triglav National Park provides an unforgettable experience.

CHAPTER FIVE
CULTURAL AND HISTORICAL HIGHLIGHTS

PTUJ

Ptuj, the oldest town in Slovenia, is a destination steeped in history, culture, and architectural charm. Nestled along the banks of the Drava River in northeastern Slovenia, Ptuj offers visitors a unique opportunity to explore Slovenia's ancient past while enjoying its vibrant traditions and relaxing atmosphere. Known for its beautifully preserved medieval center, historic landmarks, thermal spas, and lively festivals, Ptuj is a must-visit for history enthusiasts and culture seekers alike.

Ptuj's history spans over two millennia, making it one of the most historically significant towns in the country. Its origins can be traced back to the time of the Roman Empire, when it was known as Poetovio, a thriving military and trade hub. During this era, Ptuj was a key settlement along major trade routes and hosted one of the largest Roman military camps in the region. As the centuries passed, Ptuj evolved into a cultural and economic center during the medieval period, with its strategic location along the Drava River contributing to its growth and prosperity.

Today, Ptuj is a treasure trove of historical and cultural landmarks. One of its most iconic attractions is Ptuj Castle, which dominates the town from a hilltop vantage point. This beautifully preserved castle dates back to the 12th century and offers panoramic views of the town and surrounding countryside. Inside the castle, visitors can explore the Ptuj Regional Museum, which houses an impressive collection of artifacts, including medieval weapons, traditional costumes, musical instruments, and Roman relics. The museum provides a fascinating insight into the region's history and cultural heritage.

The heart of Ptuj is its Old Town, a picturesque area filled with narrow cobblestone streets, colorful buildings, and charming squares. The Town Tower, a prominent landmark, stands as a testament to Ptuj's medieval architecture and serves as a reminder of the town's rich history. Visitors can also explore the Minorite Monastery, the Dominican Monastery, and the Orpheus Monument, a Roman tombstone that is one of the oldest preserved monuments in Slovenia.

Ptuj is also famous for its vibrant traditions and festivals, the most notable of which is the Kurentovanje Carnival. This annual event, held in the weeks leading up to Lent, is one of the largest and most colorful carnivals in Slovenia. The festival features the Kurenti, traditional masked figures who perform dances and rituals to chase away winter and welcome spring. The carnival is a lively celebration of Slovenian folklore and attracts thousands of visitors from around the world.

In addition to its historical and cultural attractions, Ptuj is known for its thermal spas and wellness centers. The Ptuj Thermal Spa offers visitors a chance to relax and rejuvenate in natural thermal waters, making it a popular destination for those seeking rest and relaxation. The spa facilities include pools, saunas, and wellness treatments, providing a perfect balance to a day of sightseeing.

Wine lovers will also find much to enjoy in Ptuj, as the town is located in one of Slovenia's premier wine-producing regions. The surrounding countryside is dotted with vineyards and wineries, offering opportunities for wine tastings and tours. Ptuj's wine cellar, the Ptuj Wine Cellar, is one of the oldest in Slovenia and features a collection of excellent local wines, including the region's renowned Ljutomer Riesling and Haloze White.

For those who enjoy the outdoors, Ptuj and its surroundings offer plenty of opportunities for exploration and recreation. The Drava River is perfect for kayaking and boating, while the nearby hills and trails are ideal for hiking and cycling. The Ptuj Lake, a man-made reservoir, is another popular spot for water sports and picnicking.

Ptuj's strategic location makes it an excellent base for exploring northeastern Slovenia. It is easily accessible by road and rail and is located within a short drive of other notable destinations, such as Maribor, Jeruzalem, and the Haloze wine region.

In conclusion, Ptuj is a captivating blend of history, culture, and natural beauty. From its ancient Roman roots and medieval architecture to its lively traditions and modern wellness offerings, Ptuj provides a rich and rewarding experience for visitors. Whether you are exploring its historical landmarks, enjoying its thermal spas, or partaking in its vibrant festivals, Ptuj invites you to step back in time and discover the charm of Slovenia's oldest town.

MARIBOR AND THE WORLD'S OLDEST VINE

Maribor, Slovenia's second-largest city, is a vibrant and picturesque destination located in the heart of the Styria wine region, along the banks of the Drava River. Known for its rich history, scenic beauty, and thriving wine culture, Maribor offers a perfect blend of urban charm and natural splendor. One of its most famous attractions is the World's Oldest Vine, a living piece of history and a testament to the city's deep connection to viticulture.

Maribor's history dates back to the Middle Ages, and its old town is filled with beautifully preserved landmarks that reflect its storied past. The Lent District, the oldest part of the city, is a delightful area to explore. Its narrow streets, riverside promenade, and historic buildings create a charming atmosphere. The district is also home to the Old Vine House, where the World's Oldest Vine is located. The house serves as a museum dedicated to Slovenia's wine culture, featuring exhibits on winemaking traditions, tastings of local wines, and insights into the history of the vine.

The World's Oldest Vine, certified by the Guinness World Records, is an over 400-year-old grapevine that continues to produce fruit each year. The vine, of the Žametovka or Blauer Kolner variety, is a symbol of the city's enduring winemaking tradition and is celebrated annually with the Old Vine Festival. This event, held in the autumn, marks the grape harvest and features wine tastings, cultural performances, and culinary delights, drawing visitors from near and far.

Beyond its wine heritage, Maribor boasts numerous attractions that make it a must-visit destination. The Maribor Castle, located in the city center, houses the Regional Museum, where visitors can explore artifacts and exhibits related to the region's history, art, and culture. The Main Square (Glavni trg) is another highlight, featuring the Plague Column, a Baroque monument built in gratitude for the city's survival during the 17th-century plague epidemic.

Maribor is surrounded by stunning natural landscapes, making it an excellent destination for outdoor enthusiasts. The nearby Pohorje Hills offer year-round activities, including hiking and cycling in the warmer months and skiing in the winter. The Mariborsko Pohorje Ski Resort is one of the largest in Slovenia and hosts the renowned Golden Fox Skiing Competition, part of the FIS Alpine Ski World Cup.

Wine lovers will appreciate the many opportunities to explore the surrounding Styria wine region, which is dotted with vineyards and wine cellars. The Maribor Wine Road is a popular route, leading visitors through rolling hills and charming villages where they can sample the region's exceptional wines, such as Riesling, Furmint, and the local favorite, Šipon.

The city also offers a variety of cultural experiences, with theaters, galleries, and music festivals adding to its lively atmosphere. The annual Lent Festival, one of the largest cultural festivals in Slovenia, features performances ranging from music and dance to theater and street art, transforming Maribor into a hub of creativity and celebration.

For those seeking relaxation, Maribor provides plenty of opportunities to unwind. The Drava River is ideal for kayaking, boating, or simply strolling along its scenic banks. The city's parks and green spaces, such as Pyramid Hill (Piramida), offer peaceful retreats and beautiful views of the city and surrounding vineyards.

Maribor's central location makes it a convenient base for exploring northeastern Slovenia. It is easily accessible by road, rail, and air, with excellent connections to nearby destinations such as Ptuj, Jeruzalem, and Graz in Austria.

In conclusion, Maribor is a city that captivates with its history, wine culture, and natural beauty.

From the World's Oldest Vine and its rich winemaking traditions to the charming old town and nearby outdoor adventures, Maribor offers a diverse and memorable experience for every traveler. Whether you're savoring the region's fine wines, exploring its historical landmarks, or enjoying its vibrant festivals, Maribor invites you to discover the unique charm of Slovenia's Styria region.

CULTURAL FESTIVALS AND TRADITIONS

Slovenia is a country rich in cultural heritage, and its festivals and traditions reflect a vibrant blend of history, folklore, and modern creativity. Throughout the year, Slovenia hosts a variety of cultural events that showcase its unique identity, celebrate its customs, and bring communities together. From centuries-old rituals to contemporary festivals, these events offer visitors a chance to experience the heart of Slovenian culture.

Slovenia's cultural calendar begins with Kurentovanje, one of the country's most famous and colorful traditions. Held in Ptuj, this carnival is a pre-Lenten celebration rooted in ancient pagan customs. The highlight of Kurentovanje is the appearance of the Kurenti, masked figures adorned with sheepskins, cowbells, and colorful ribbons who perform lively dances to chase away winter and welcome spring. This UNESCO-recognized tradition is a lively blend of parades, music, and folklore, drawing thousands of visitors each year.

Ljubljana, Slovenia's capital, is a hub of cultural festivals. The Ljubljana Festival, held in the summer, is one of the country's most prestigious events, featuring world-class performances in music, theater, and dance. The festival attracts renowned artists and ensembles from around the globe, transforming the city into a cultural hotspot. Other notable events include the Ljubljana Jazz Festival, which celebrates the best of Slovenian and international jazz, and the Animateka Festival, dedicated to animated films and visual storytelling.

In the wine-rich region of Maribor, the Old Vine Festival is a highlight of the autumn season. This festival celebrates the World's Oldest Vine, a symbol of Maribor's viticultural heritage, and features wine tastings, culinary events, and traditional music. The festival is a tribute to Slovenia's deep connection with winemaking and offers visitors a chance to savor the flavors of the Styria wine region.

Bled, known for its enchanting lake and castle, hosts the Bled Days and Nights Festival in the summer. This event includes concerts, art exhibitions, and the spectacular Lake Bled Lights, where thousands of floating candles illuminate the water, creating a magical atmosphere. Another charming tradition in Bled is the Pletna Boat Ceremony, showcasing the skills of local rowers who guide traditional wooden boats across the lake.

In Idrija, the art of lace-making takes center stage during the Idrija Lace Festival, which celebrates the town's centuries-old craft. Visitors can admire intricate lacework, participate in workshops, and learn about the history of this

UNESCO-inscribed tradition. The festival also includes cultural performances and local culinary delights.

Slovenia's Pohorje Hills and Julian Alps regions celebrate their pastoral heritage with traditional events like the Cow Ball Festival in Bohinj. This end-of-summer celebration marks the return of cattle from mountain pastures and features folk music, dancing, and demonstrations of local customs such as cheese-making.

The country's coastal towns, such as Piran and Koper, host maritime festivals that highlight Slovenia's seafaring traditions. The Salt Festival in Piran celebrates the historic salt-making industry, with salt-related activities, traditional music, and local seafood specialties. Similarly, the Fisherman's Festival in Izola offers a lively mix of concerts, culinary events, and boat rides.

Religious festivals also play an important role in Slovenian culture. Easter, Christmas, and All Saints' Day are marked by traditional rituals, processions, and special foods. In rural areas, these celebrations often incorporate elements of Slovenian folklore, such as Easter egg painting (pisanice) and nativity scenes crafted by local artisans.

Modern Slovenia embraces contemporary culture through events like the Fabula Literature Festival, which brings together writers and thinkers from around the world, and the Sonica Festival, focusing on experimental music and multimedia art. These festivals highlight Slovenia's commitment to innovation and creativity in the arts.

Slovenia's traditions are deeply connected to its natural environment, and many festivals celebrate the changing seasons and rural life. Harvest festivals, grape-picking celebrations, and mushroom festivals reflect the country's agricultural roots and provide a window into local life.

In every corner of Slovenia, cultural festivals and traditions bring the nation's history, creativity, and community spirit to life. Whether you're enjoying the ancient rituals of Kurentovanje, the elegance of a lace-making demonstration, or the modern beats of a music festival, these events offer an authentic and enriching experience of Slovenia's diverse cultural identity.

MUSEUMS AND ART GALLERIES

Slovenia boasts a rich collection of museums and art galleries that reflect its vibrant cultural heritage, artistic innovation, and historical significance. These institutions offer visitors a deep dive into the country's art, history, science, and unique traditions, making them essential stops for any cultural itinerary. From ancient artifacts to cutting-edge contemporary art, Slovenia's museums and galleries provide something for everyone.

The National Museum of Slovenia in Ljubljana is the country's oldest museum and a treasure trove of archaeological and historical artifacts. Highlights include the Venus of Dolní Věstonice, a Paleolithic figurine, and the world's oldest musical instrument, a Neanderthal flute carved from a bear's femur. The museum's exhibits span Slovenia's history, from prehistory to the present, offering a comprehensive view of its cultural evolution.

Art enthusiasts will appreciate the National Gallery of Slovenia, also located in Ljubljana. This museum houses the country's most extensive collection of visual art, featuring works by Slovenian and European masters. Highlights include Medieval frescoes, Baroque paintings, and 19th-century Romantic art by Slovenian painters such as Ivana Kobilca and Jožef Tominc. The gallery's modern wing also hosts temporary exhibitions that showcase contemporary art trends.

The Museum of Modern Art in Ljubljana is a hub for 20th- and 21st-century Slovenian and international art. Its collection features works by notable Slovenian modernists, including Zoran Mušič and Marij Pregelj, alongside contemporary pieces that explore themes of identity, politics, and technology. The museum frequently collaborates with international artists, making it a dynamic space for art exploration.

Metelkova Museum Quarter, a cultural complex in Ljubljana, includes the Slovenian Ethnographic Museum and the Museum of Contemporary Art Metelkova (MSUM). The Ethnographic Museum offers an insightful look at Slovenia's folk traditions, including exhibits on traditional costumes, crafts, and everyday life.

MSUM focuses on avant-garde and experimental art, housing a significant collection of contemporary works from Slovenia and the former Yugoslav region.

In Ptuj, the Ptuj Ormož Regional Museum offers a journey through the region's rich history. Located in the iconic Ptuj Castle, the museum showcases Roman artifacts, medieval weaponry, and traditional Slovenian costumes. Visitors can also explore the castle's beautifully preserved interiors, including the impressive knight's hall and Baroque salons.

Maribor, Slovenia's second-largest city, is home to the Regional Museum Maribor, located in the Maribor Castle. The museum presents the history of the city and the surrounding Styria region, featuring artifacts from the Roman period, medieval manuscripts, and an extensive collection of folk art. The UGM Maribor Art

Gallery is another highlight, with a focus on modern and contemporary Slovenian art.

The Technical Museum of Slovenia, situated in Bistra, near Ljubljana, is a fascinating destination for science and technology enthusiasts. Located in a former monastery, the museum features exhibits on Slovenia's industrial heritage, transportation, woodworking, and agriculture. Highlights include vintage cars, including one used by Marshal Tito, and interactive displays that appeal to visitors of all ages.

For a unique museum experience, the Kobarid Museum in the Soča Valley focuses on World War I and the infamous Isonzo Front battles. The museum's detailed exhibits and multimedia presentations provide a moving account of the hardships faced by soldiers and civilians during this tumultuous time. The nearby Fort Kluže, a historic military fortification, complements the museum's narrative.

In the picturesque town of Idrija, the Idrija Municipal Museum at Gewerkenegg Castle celebrates the region's mining heritage and lace-making traditions. Exhibits detail the history of mercury mining, for which Idrija is a UNESCO World Heritage Site, as well as the artistry of Idrija lace, a craft with centuries-old roots.

Coastal Slovenia offers cultural gems such as the Sergej Mašera Maritime Museum in Piran, which explores the region's maritime history through exhibits on shipbuilding, navigation, and local fishing traditions. The Piran Coastal Galleries present contemporary art inspired by the Adriatic environment, providing a modern perspective on the coastal lifestyle.

For those intrigued by Slovenia's natural history, the Slovenian Museum of Natural History in Ljubljana showcases fascinating exhibits on geology, paleontology, and biodiversity. Highlights include the skeletal remains of a woolly mammoth and an impressive mineral collection.

Art lovers seeking alternative spaces can explore the vibrant street art scene at Metelkova Mesto in Ljubljana. This autonomous cultural zone is a living gallery, with murals, sculptures, and installations adorning its buildings. It also hosts exhibitions, concerts, and workshops, making it a dynamic hub for creativity.

In conclusion, Slovenia's museums and art galleries reflect the nation's rich tapestry of history, art, and culture. From ancient treasures to contemporary masterpieces, these institutions offer diverse experiences that celebrate Slovenia's past and present. Whether you're captivated by medieval artifacts, fascinated by modern art, or drawn to the stories of everyday life, Slovenia's cultural spaces invite you to discover its soul through its artistic and historical treasures.

CHAPTER SIX

NATURE AND OUTDOOR ACTIVITIES

EXPLORING THE JULIAN ALPS

Exploring the Julian Alps is an unforgettable adventure into one of Europe's most stunning mountain ranges, where dramatic peaks, glacial valleys, alpine meadows, and pristine lakes create a breathtaking landscape. Located in northwestern Slovenia, the Julian Alps form part of the southern range of the Alps and are home to Triglav National Park, Slovenia's only national park, named after Mount Triglav, the country's highest peak and national symbol. This region offers a diverse array of activities, from hiking and mountaineering to cultural exploration and wildlife spotting, making it a must-visit destination for nature enthusiasts and adventure seekers.

The Julian Alps are characterized by their rugged limestone peaks, deep gorges, and emerald-green rivers. Mount Triglav, standing at 2,864 meters (9,396 feet), is a highlight for many visitors. Climbing Triglav is considered a rite of passage for Slovenians, and it attracts climbers and hikers from around the world. The ascent, while challenging, is achievable for experienced hikers and offers panoramic views of the surrounding peaks and valleys.

For those seeking less strenuous but equally rewarding hikes, the Julian Alps offer a vast network of trails suitable for all levels. The Seven Lakes Valley is one of the most iconic routes, winding through picturesque alpine lakes surrounded by dramatic cliffs and lush greenery. Other popular trails include the Pokljuka Plateau, known for its dense spruce forests and charming mountain pastures, and the Vršič Pass, Slovenia's highest mountain pass, which provides stunning views of the Soča Valley and the rugged peaks of the Julian Alps.

The region is also renowned for its pristine alpine lakes. Lake Bled, with its emerald waters and iconic island church, is a picture-perfect destination that draws visitors year-round. Nearby, Lake Bohinj, the largest natural lake in Slovenia, offers a quieter and more serene atmosphere. Surrounded by the Julian Alps, Lake Bohinj is ideal for swimming, kayaking, and paddleboarding in the summer, as well as ice skating in the winter.

The Soča River, often called the "Emerald River," is another jewel of the Julian Alps. Its vibrant turquoise waters flow through the Soča Valley, offering opportunities for white-water rafting, kayaking, and fishing. The valley is also home to charming villages, such as Kobarid and Bovec, which serve as excellent bases for outdoor adventures. The Kobarid Museum, dedicated to World War I history, and the nearby Tolmin Gorges, with their dramatic rock formations and crystal-clear pools, are must-visit attractions in the area.

Winter transforms the Julian Alps into a paradise for snow sports enthusiasts. The Vogel Ski Resort, located above Lake Bohinj, offers spectacular views and excellent slopes for skiing and snowboarding. Other popular resorts include Kranjska Gora, known for its family-friendly atmosphere and hosting events like the FIS Alpine Ski World Cup, and Kanin-Sella Nevea, which features cross-border skiing between Slovenia and Italy.

Beyond natural beauty, the Julian Alps are steeped in culture and tradition. The alpine villages scattered throughout the region are known for their warm hospitality, traditional architecture, and local cuisine. Visitors can sample hearty dishes such as žganci (buckwheat porridge), bovški sir (Bovec cheese), and jota (a comforting bean and sauerkraut stew). Local mountain huts, or planinske koče, provide cozy accommodations and meals for hikers, often offering stunning views of the surrounding peaks.

The Julian Alps are also a haven for biodiversity. The park is home to a wide variety of flora and fauna, including edelweiss, chamois, ibex, and golden eagles. Wildlife enthusiasts may spot these creatures while exploring the park's trails, especially in the more remote areas. The rich ecosystem and pristine environment make this region a vital part of Slovenia's natural heritage.

For those interested in history, the Julian Alps bear the scars of World War I, particularly in the Isonzo Front, where fierce battles were fought between Austro-Hungarian and Italian forces. Historical trails, such as the Walk of Peace, connect key sites, including trenches, forts, and memorials, offering insights into the region's wartime history and its impact on the local landscape and communities.

In addition to its outdoor adventures and cultural experiences, the Julian Alps offer opportunities for relaxation and wellness. Thermal spas in nearby towns, such as Bled and Bohinj, provide a soothing retreat after a day of exploration, with facilities that include thermal pools, saunas, and massages.

In conclusion, the Julian Alps are a destination of extraordinary beauty and diversity. Whether you're hiking through alpine meadows, skiing down snow-covered slopes, paddling on turquoise lakes, or simply soaking in the tranquility of the mountain landscape, the Julian Alps promise an unforgettable journey into the heart of Slovenia's natural and cultural wonders.

SOCA VALLEY

The Soča Valley, located in the western part of Slovenia, is a region of extraordinary natural beauty, rich history, and endless adventure. At its heart lies the Soča River, a stunning turquoise waterway often referred to as "The Emerald Beauty." This river originates in the Julian Alps and winds its way through lush valleys and dramatic gorges, making it one of the most beautiful rivers in Europe. Its crystal-clear waters are perfect for activities like kayaking, rafting, fly fishing, and swimming, while its picturesque scenery attracts visitors from all over the world. Alongside the river runs the Soča Trail, a scenic walking path that connects many of the valley's highlights and offers breathtaking views of the landscape.

The valley is also home to some of Slovenia's most iconic waterfalls. The Boka Waterfall, the tallest in the country, captivates visitors with its sheer power and height. Other waterfalls, like the serene Virje Waterfall and the mystical Kozjak Waterfall hidden within a cavern-like gorge, add to the region's charm and are must-see destinations for nature lovers.

Outdoor enthusiasts will find the Soča Valley a haven for adventure. Whitewater rafting and kayaking are among the most popular activities, offering thrilling experiences on the river's rapids. Canyoning in the valley's tributary streams provides an adrenaline-pumping descent through waterfalls and natural pools. Hiking is another major draw, with trails that cater to all levels, from easy riverside walks to challenging alpine climbs. The Alpe-Adria Trail, an international hiking route, passes through the valley, showcasing its breathtaking beauty. Cyclists can explore the valley on scenic routes, while mountain bikers will enjoy the challenging paths along Kobariški Stol and Kolovrat Ridge. For those seeking an aerial perspective, paragliding over the valley's dramatic peaks and emerald river offers an unforgettable experience.

The Soča Valley is dotted with charming towns and villages that serve as gateways to its attractions. Bovec, known as the adventure capital of Slovenia, is a lively town where outdoor activities abound. Kobarid, a picturesque and historically significant town, is famous for its role in World War I and its excellent Kobarid Museum, which offers a moving account of the Isonzo Front. Tolmin, located at the southern end of the valley, is renowned for the Tolmin Gorges, a natural wonder featuring narrow canyons and crystal-clear pools that enchant visitors with their beauty.

The region's historical significance is deeply tied to the events of World War I, particularly the Isonzo Front. The Walk of Peace, a network of trails and memorials, connects significant battlefields, cemeteries, and fortifications, preserving the memory of this tumultuous period. The Kobarid Museum provides an in-depth look at the war's impact on the region, displaying artifacts, photographs, and personal accounts that tell the story of the soldiers and civilians who lived through it.

Cultural richness is another hallmark of the Soča Valley. Visitors can experience traditional Slovenian cuisine, including dishes like frika, a cheese and potato specialty, and bovški krafi, sweet dumplings unique to the area. Local trout from the Soča River is also a delicacy. Festivals and events, such as the Soča Outdoor Festival and the Shepherds' Festival in Bovec, celebrate the region's heritage and bring the community together.

The valley's natural environment is part of Triglav National Park, which ensures the conservation of its unique ecosystems. Wildlife enthusiasts may encounter chamois, ibex, golden eagles, and other species that thrive in the surrounding forests and alpine meadows. The park's dedication to sustainability helps preserve this pristine wilderness for future generations.

The Soča Valley is easily accessible by car or bus from major Slovenian cities, and the scenic Bohinj Railway offers a unique way to experience the area. Accommodations range from luxury hotels and charming guesthouses to campgrounds and mountain huts, providing options for every traveler. Late spring, summer, and early autumn are ideal times to visit for outdoor activities, while winter offers a quieter experience with opportunities for skiing and snowshoeing.

The Soča Valley is a destination of unparalleled beauty, adventure, and history. Its turquoise waters, majestic peaks, and charming villages make it an unforgettable place to explore. Whether you're rafting down the Soča River, hiking its scenic trails, or immersing yourself in its wartime past, the valley promises a journey filled with awe and inspiration.

CAVES AND KARST LANDSCAPES

Slovenia's caves and karst landscapes are among the most remarkable natural wonders in Europe, offering breathtaking subterranean worlds and dramatic surface features shaped over millions of years. Situated in the southwestern region of the country, the karst terrain is a geological marvel characterized by limestone plateaus, underground rivers, sinkholes, and vast cave systems. These features have earned Slovenia its nickname as the "Land of Karst" and attract visitors eager to explore its unique beauty.

The most famous cave in Slovenia is Postojna Cave, a 24,000-meter-long system of underground passages, galleries, and chambers. It is one of the largest and most visited show caves in the world. The journey into Postojna Cave begins with an iconic electric train ride, taking visitors deep into a mesmerizing underground world filled with stalactites, stalagmites, and flowstone formations. Highlights include the Brilliant, a sparkling white stalagmite that has become a symbol of the cave, and the Concert Hall, a massive chamber known for its excellent acoustics and occasional performances. Postojna Cave is also home to the olm or "human fish," a unique amphibian species that has adapted to its dark environment.

Another must-visit karst wonder is Škocjan Caves, a UNESCO World Heritage Site renowned for its immense underground canyon. The Škocjan Caves offer a dramatic experience as visitors traverse high bridges above roaring subterranean rivers and marvel at awe-inspiring rock formations. This cave system is also an important archaeological and ecological site, showcasing the power of natural forces in shaping the landscape.

Predjama Castle, located near Postojna, combines history and geology in a fascinating way. This medieval castle is dramatically perched at the mouth of a cave on a towering cliff. Exploring Predjama Castle reveals hidden passageways, secret chambers, and stories of the legendary knight Erazem Lueger, who used the castle as his fortress.

Beyond the major attractions, Slovenia is dotted with smaller, equally stunning caves. Križna Cave is celebrated for its tranquil underground lakes, which visitors can explore by boat, and its pristine, untouched beauty. Vilenica Cave, one of Europe's oldest tourist caves, offers a more intimate experience with its intricate rock formations and mythical folklore. For adventure seekers, Pivka and Black Caves provide a wilder, less commercialized caving experience.

The karst landscape above ground is equally fascinating. Features like sinkholes, karst poljes (seasonal fields that flood), and disappearing streams create a dynamic and ever-changing terrain. The Rak Škocjan Valley, a picturesque karst valley, is ideal for hiking and exploring natural stone bridges, springs, and caves. Planina Polje, another karst field, is a hotspot for speleologists and nature enthusiasts alike.

Slovenia's karst region is also the birthplace of the scientific study of karst phenomena, and the term "karst" itself originates from the Kras Plateau in this area. Visitors can learn more about the unique geology and history of karst at the Karst Museum in Postojna or through guided tours that delve into the science and folklore of the region.

Wine lovers will appreciate the karst region's connection to the Teran wine, a robust red wine produced in the area's iron-rich soils. Paired with traditional karst prosciutto, this culinary specialty is a perfect way to experience the cultural heritage of the region.

The caves and karst landscapes of Slovenia are not only geological treasures but also windows into the country's history, culture, and biodiversity. From awe-inspiring cave tours and adventurous expeditions to serene hikes and culinary delights, these features make Slovenia a top destination for nature enthusiasts and explorers.

SLOVENIAN WINE REGIONS

Slovenia, though small in size, boasts a rich and ancient winemaking tradition that dates back over 2,400 years. Its diverse geography, microclimates, and soils contribute to an impressive variety of wines, many of which are internationally acclaimed. With three distinct wine regions—Podravje, Primorska, and Posavje—Slovenia offers something for every wine lover, from crisp whites to bold reds and unique orange wines.

- Podravje Wine Region

Located in northeastern Slovenia, Podravje is the country's largest and most renowned wine region, particularly for its white wines. The cool climate and fertile soils make it ideal for producing elegant, aromatic wines with vibrant acidity.

This region is divided into two sub-regions: Štajerska Slovenija (Styria Slovenia) and Prekmurje. Štajerska is celebrated for its Riesling, Sauvignon Blanc, Chardonnay, and Furmint (Šipon), while Prekmurje produces some unique dessert wines and sparkling varieties. Podravje is also famous for haložan, a refreshing blend traditionally enjoyed in local taverns.

One of the highlights of Podravje is Jeruzalem, a picturesque wine-growing area with rolling hills and vineyards that date back to Roman times.

Jeruzalem is not only a wine paradise but also offers stunning views and a rich cultural experience.

- Primorska Wine Region

Situated in western Slovenia near the Adriatic Sea, Primorska is known for its full-bodied red wines, as well as distinctive whites and orange wines. This Mediterranean-influenced region is divided into four sub-regions: Goriška Brda, Vipava Valley, Kras, and Slovenska Istra.

Goriška Brda, often referred to as "Slovenian Tuscany," is famous for its high-quality wines, such as Merlot, Cabernet Sauvignon, and the indigenous white grape variety Rebula (Ribolla Gialla). The Brda region is a favorite for wine tourism, offering charming villages, boutique wineries, and breathtaking views of vineyards stretching into Italy.

The Vipava Valley is a windswept area producing aromatic whites like Pinela and Zelen, two rare local varieties. Its reds, such as Barbera and Merlot, are equally noteworthy. The valley's wineries are known for their innovative winemaking techniques and embrace of organic and biodynamic practices.

The Kras Plateau is the home of Teran, a robust red wine made from the indigenous Refosco grape. The region's iron-rich "terra rossa" soil gives Teran its characteristic boldness and minerality. Pairing Teran with traditional karst prosciutto is a must for visitors.

Slovenska Istra, located along the coast, specializes in Mediterranean wines like Malvasia and Refosco, as well as olive oil and truffles. The coastal breezes and sunny climate imbue the wines with a unique, refreshing quality.

- Posavje Wine Region

Situated in southeastern Slovenia, Posavje is the smallest of the three regions and is particularly known for its Cviček, a light and low-alcohol red blend that is unique to Slovenia. Cviček, made primarily from red and white grape varieties, is refreshing, slightly tart, and pairs well with traditional Slovenian dishes.

Posavje comprises three sub-regions: Dolenjska, Bela Krajina, and Bizeljsko-Sremič. Dolenjska is the birthplace of Cviček and also produces Metliška Črnina, a soft red wine. Bela Krajina is known for its white wines like Belokranjec and traditional vineyard cottages. Bizeljsko-Sremič stands out for its sparkling wines and unique repnice (wine cellars carved into siliceous sand).

- Wine Tourism in Slovenia

Wine tourism is thriving in Slovenia, with numerous wineries offering tastings, tours, and accommodations. Many regions host wine festivals and events throughout the year, such as the St. Martin's Day celebrations in November, which mark the traditional turning of grape juice into wine. Visitors can also explore wine roads that meander through scenic vineyards and charming villages, each offering an authentic Slovenian wine experience.

- Notable Wine Styles

Slovenia is a pioneer in the production of orange wines, made by fermenting white grapes with their skins. This ancient winemaking method has gained international acclaim, especially in the Primorska region. Additionally, the country excels in producing sparkling wines, dessert wines, and natural wines, reflecting its innovative and diverse winemaking culture.

- Why Slovenian Wine Stands Out

Slovenia's small-scale, family-run wineries focus on quality and sustainability. Many vineyards practice organic or biodynamic farming, respecting the environment and traditional methods. With over 50 distinct grape varieties, including indigenous ones like Rebula, Teran, Pinela, and Šipon, Slovenian wines offer a unique flavor profile that reflects the country's diverse terroir.

Slovenia's wine regions are a testament to the country's rich winemaking heritage, breathtaking landscapes, and dedication to quality. Whether exploring the rolling hills of Podravje, the sun-soaked vineyards of Primorska, or the quaint traditions of Posavje, wine lovers are sure to be enchanted by Slovenia's vibrant and flavorful offerings.

CHAPTER SEVEN

FOOD AND CULINARY EXPERIENCES

TRADITIONAL SLOVENIAN CUISINE

Traditional Slovenian cuisine is a delightful reflection of the country's diverse landscapes, rich history, and cultural influences from its neighbors—Italy, Austria, Hungary, and the Balkans. The cuisine emphasizes fresh, local, and seasonal ingredients, offering a mix of hearty comfort foods and refined flavors. Each region has its specialties, making Slovenian gastronomy as varied as its geography.

- Key Ingredients and Influences

Slovenian cuisine is shaped by its natural resources, with ingredients sourced from fertile valleys, alpine pastures, karst regions, and the

Adriatic coast. Staples include potatoes, grains, beans, dairy products, pork, and seasonal vegetables. Wild herbs, mushrooms, and honey often enhance dishes. Proximity to neighboring countries has introduced flavors like Italian risottos, Austrian schnitzels, and Hungarian goulash into Slovenian cooking, while still maintaining its unique identity.

- Iconic Slovenian Dishes

1. Žganci: A traditional dish made from buckwheat or cornmeal, žganci is a rustic staple often served with sour milk, sausages, or stews. Its simplicity and versatility make it a beloved comfort food.

2. Potica: Potica is Slovenia's most famous dessert, a rolled pastry filled with various ingredients such as walnuts, poppy seeds, honey, or tarragon. It is traditionally prepared during holidays and celebrations and is a symbol of Slovenian heritage.

3. Štruklji: Štruklji are rolled dumplings filled with savory or sweet fillings, such as cottage cheese, nuts, apples, or herbs. They can be baked, boiled, or steamed and are enjoyed as a side dish, dessert, or main course.

4. Kranjska Klobasa: This traditional Carniolan sausage is made from pork, bacon, garlic, and spices, encased in natural skin and smoked. It is a protected product with a unique recipe that dates back centuries and is often served with sauerkraut or mustard.

5. Jota: Jota is a hearty stew made from sauerkraut or turnip, beans, potatoes, and sometimes pork. This warming dish is a staple in Primorska and other regions, especially during the colder months.

6. Bograč: Inspired by Hungarian goulash, bograč is a rich meat stew prepared with three types of meat (typically pork, beef, and

venison), potatoes, and paprika. It is particularly popular in Prekmurje.

7. Bled Cream Cake (Blejska Kremšnita): A signature dessert of Lake Bled, this creamy treat features layers of puff pastry and vanilla custard topped with whipped cream. It is a must-try for visitors to the region.

8. Idrijski Žlikrofi: These small dumplings, filled with potato and onion, are a specialty of the town of Idrija. They are often served with a meat sauce or as a side dish to stews. Idrijski žlikrofi are protected as a traditional specialty of Slovenia.

9. Frika: Frika is a cheese-and-potato dish from the Soča Valley and western Slovenia. It is typically pan-fried until crispy and golden and served with polenta or salad.

10. Prekmurska Gibanica: This layered pastry from Prekmurje combines poppy seeds, cottage cheese, walnuts, and apples, creating a decadent dessert with a harmonious blend of textures and flavors.

11. Ričet: A wholesome barley stew cooked with beans, potatoes, and vegetables, ričet is a traditional Slovenian dish often flavored with smoked meat or sausage.

12. Šelinka: A celery-based soup, Šelinka is simple yet flavorful, often served with potatoes or as a starter in many households.

13. Coastal and Karst Specialties: The Primorska region offers Mediterranean-inspired dishes like fish stew (brodet), squid, and octopus salad. The Karst Plateau is famous for karst prosciutto (pršut), aged in the region's unique climate, and the robust red wine

Teran, which pairs perfectly with the prosciutto.

- Beverages
1. Slovenian Wines: Slovenia's wine culture is deeply rooted in tradition, with three main wine regions—Podravje, Primorska, and Posavje—producing exceptional white, red, and orange wines. Local varieties like Rebula, Teran, and Šipon are celebrated.

2. Slovenian Beers: Craft brewing is on the rise in Slovenia, adding to the appeal of traditional lagers from renowned breweries like Union and Laško.

3. Herbal Liqueurs and Spirits: Traditional spirits like schnapps (žganje), made from fruits like pears, plums, or apples, and herbal liqueurs such as teranov liker, are popular. The honey-flavored medica is a sweet favorite.

4. Mineral Water: Slovenia's natural springs provide high-quality mineral waters, including the internationally recognized Donat Mg, rich in magnesium.

- Farm-to-Table and Culinary Heritage

Slovenia takes pride in its commitment to sustainable and local food. Many traditional dishes are made using ingredients sourced from family farms, local markets, and wild foraging. Gostilnas (traditional inns) offer authentic home-cooked meals that reflect the region's flavors and culinary traditions. The country's embrace of slow food and its designation as the 2021 European Region of Gastronomy showcase its dedication to preserving and promoting its rich food heritage.

Traditional Slovenian cuisine is a celebration of the country's natural bounty, cultural diversity, and culinary artistry. From hearty stews and sausages to delicate pastries and world-class wines, Slovenia offers a dining experience that delights the palate and connects visitors to its deep-rooted traditions.

BEST RESTAURANTS ACROSS THE COUNTRY

Slovenia's culinary scene is a vibrant blend of tradition and innovation, with restaurants ranging from cozy inns serving traditional dishes to Michelin-starred establishments redefining fine dining. Each region offers its own specialties, and the country's dedication to local, seasonal, and sustainable ingredients ensures a remarkable dining experience.

In Ljubljana, the capital city, a range of restaurants highlight both traditional Slovenian dishes and modern gastronomy. Hiša Franko, located in Kobarid, is one of the most renowned restaurants in the country and the world. Led by Ana Roš, a celebrated chef, it focuses on hyperlocal ingredients and the flavors of the Soča Valley. JB Restaurant, in the heart of Ljubljana, offers an elegant approach to Slovenian cuisine, crafted by Chef Janez Bratovž, a pioneer of the country's fine dining scene. Gostilna As combines Mediterranean influences with modern Slovenian flavors, creating a sophisticated dining experience, while Atelje, a Michelin-starred gem, emphasizes simplicity and creativity using seasonal ingredients.

In the Primorska region, Mediterranean-inspired dishes take center stage. Hiša Torkla, in Korte, offers exquisite grilled meats and regional specialties with breathtaking views of the Istrian countryside. Gostilna Pri Lojzetu, housed in Zemono Manor near Vipava, is a Michelin-starred destination where Chef Tomaž Kavčič blends traditional recipes with innovative techniques. Rizibizi, in Portorož, is celebrated for its contemporary take on seafood and coastal flavors.

Štajerska and Prekmurje, in northeastern Slovenia, are known for hearty, locally inspired meals. Restavracija Mak in Maribor stands out with its bold and artistic approach to Slovenian gastronomy, crafted by Chef David Vračko. Gostilna Rajh in Murska Sobota highlights traditional Prekmurje cuisine, including dishes like Prekmurska gibanica and bograč stew, all prepared with a modern twist.

In the Alpine Gorenjska region, dining reflects the comfort and richness of mountain life. Gostilna Pri Planincu in Bled serves generous portions of Slovenian favorites, including the iconic Bled cream cake. Gostilna Kunstelj, in Radovljica, offers dishes made from its own garden, paired with stunning views of the Julian Alps.

The Karst and Soča Valley regions are known for their bold, earthy flavors and high-quality local ingredients. Gostilna Križman in Tomaj showcases regional specialties such as karst prosciutto and robust stews. Restavracija Topli Val in Kobarid emphasizes fresh trout and other delicacies inspired by the pristine Soča River.

In the Posavje region, the culinary traditions are simple yet deeply flavorful. Gostilna Repovž in Šentjanž combines farm-to-table dining with dishes inspired by the area's rich heritage, using ingredients from their family farm.

Unique dining experiences can be found throughout the country. Domačija Novak in Dolenjska offers rustic charm with expertly prepared dishes like štruklji and wild mushroom soup. Kendov Dvorec in Idrija provides a historic and refined setting to enjoy heritage-inspired cuisine.

Slovenia's restaurants often feature deep connections to local wineries, offering perfectly curated wine pairings that highlight the harmony between food and wine. From sipping Rebula with fresh seafood in Primorska to enjoying Šipon with a delicate dessert in Podravje, Slovenian gastronomy celebrates this symbiotic relationship.

Whether at a Michelin-starred restaurant, a traditional gostilna, or a scenic vineyard eatery, Slovenia's dining experiences are infused with creativity, tradition, and passion. Each meal is a journey through the country's diverse landscapes and culinary heritage, leaving visitors with unforgettable flavors and memories.

WINE TASTING IN SLOVENIA'S VINEYARDS

Wine tasting in Slovenia's vineyards is an unforgettable experience, offering a chance to explore the country's rich wine heritage, stunning landscapes, and warm hospitality. With a winemaking tradition that dates back thousands of years, Slovenia boasts three major wine regions Podravje, Primorska, and Posavje—each with its unique varieties and character. Known for producing high-quality white, red, and orange wines, Slovenia is a hidden gem for wine enthusiasts.

The experience of wine tasting in Slovenia often includes visits to boutique wineries, family-run vineyards, and traditional wine cellars. Many wineries pride themselves on sustainable and biodynamic practices, focusing on natural processes that preserve the essence of the region. Wine tastings are often accompanied by local foods such as cheeses, cured meats, and breads, offering a full sensory journey.

The Primorska region, located in western Slovenia near the Adriatic coast, is heavily influenced by Mediterranean flavors and is renowned for its robust red wines and crisp whites. The Vipava Valley, within this region, offers an ideal climate for growing unique grape varieties like Zelen and Pinela. Visitors to the valley can enjoy tastings at wineries such as Tilia Estate and Burja Estate, where traditional and modern techniques merge seamlessly. The Goriška Brda subregion, often referred to as "Slovenia's Tuscany," is famous for its Rebula and Merlot wines. Boutique wineries like Klet Brda and Movia offer intimate tasting experiences with panoramic views of rolling vineyards.

In the northeastern region of Podravje, the focus shifts to elegant white wines and sweet varieties. The Štajerska subregion is Slovenia's largest wine-producing area and is known for its Laski Riesling, Sauvignon Blanc, and Traminer. Wineries like Ptujska Klet, the oldest wine cellar in Slovenia, and Radgonske Gorice, famous for sparkling wines, provide exceptional tasting experiences. The Jeruzalem-Ormož Hills are another highlight, where the scenic vineyards and crisp whites, including Šipon (Furmint), create a magical ambiance.

The Posavje region, located in southeastern Slovenia, is celebrated for its unique red blend, Cviček, which is light, low in alcohol, and refreshingly distinct. The Bizeljsko-Sremič Hills offer a mix of sparkling wines and full-bodied reds, while the Dolenjska subregion is perfect for exploring Cviček's heritage. Wineries such as Istenič and Frelih offer guided tastings and insights into local winemaking traditions.

Slovenian wineries often emphasize slow-paced, personalized tours. Winemakers enjoy sharing stories about their family traditions and the passion behind each bottle. Many vineyards also offer accommodation options, providing the opportunity to stay among the vines and enjoy breathtaking sunsets paired with a glass of wine.

Wine festivals are another way to immerse yourself in Slovenia's wine culture. Events like the Ljubljana Wine Route and the St. Martin's Day celebrations, held across the country in November, allow visitors to sample a variety of wines and learn about Slovenia's vinicultural history.

Wine tasting in Slovenia is not just about the flavors in the glass but also the journey through picturesque landscapes, historic cellars, and the warm company of local winemakers. From the Mediterranean breezes of Primorska to the lush hills of Podravje and Posavje, Slovenia offers an authentic and enchanting wine experience that appeals to novices and connoisseurs alike.

LOCAL MARKETS AND FARM-TO-TABLE DINING

Local markets and farm-to-table dining in Slovenia offer an authentic way to experience the country's vibrant culinary culture and commitment to sustainability. Slovenia's rich agricultural heritage, diverse landscapes, and dedication to preserving traditional farming methods create a thriving food scene that celebrates fresh, seasonal, and locally sourced ingredients. Whether visiting bustling city markets or savoring meals in rustic countryside inns, these experiences immerse you in the heart of Slovenian gastronomy.

- Local Markets

Slovenian markets are a sensory delight, filled with colorful produce, artisan products, and a lively atmosphere. These markets are not just places to shop but also social hubs where locals and visitors connect over food and stories.

The Central Market in Ljubljana, designed by the famed architect Jože Plečnik, is one of the most iconic. It stretches along the Ljubljanica River and features a covered arcade, open-air stalls, and a vibrant marketplace. Here, you'll find everything from fresh fruits and vegetables to honey, herbs, flowers, and handmade crafts. On Fridays, the market transforms into Odprta Kuhna (Open Kitchen), where local chefs and food vendors serve dishes from Slovenia and beyond.

In Maribor, the Main Market Square (Glavni Trg) showcases the agricultural bounty of the Štajerska region. Visitors can sample fresh apples, pumpkin seeds, and oils, which are specialties of the area. Smaller towns like Piran, Koper, and Ptuj also host charming farmers' markets offering regional produce and seafood.

The Mercado in Piran is especially notable for its selection of Adriatic seafood, while markets in Prekmurje and the Karst region highlight specialty items such as dried fruits, cheeses, and prosciutto.

- Farm-to-Table Dining

Slovenia's farm-to-table dining scene reflects its commitment to sustainability and local traditions. Many gostilnas (traditional inns) and modern restaurants collaborate directly with farmers, foragers, and producers to create menus that tell the story of the land.

Gostilna Repovž in the Posavje region epitomizes farm-to-table dining. Their dishes feature ingredients sourced from their own farm and local suppliers, offering a menu rooted in regional flavors. Similarly, Hiša Franko, run by world-renowned chef Ana Roš, sources its ingredients from the surrounding Soča Valley, creating avant-garde dishes that celebrate local biodiversity.

The Karst region is famous for karst prosciutto (pršut) and Teran wine, often served in family-run inns like Gostilna Križman, where traditional recipes meet modern hospitality. In the Vipava

Valley, farm-to-table experiences include visits to vineyards and orchards that supply the restaurants with fresh produce and wines.

In the Štajerska region, Restavracija Mak in Maribor focuses on hyperlocal ingredients, blending bold flavors with artistic presentation. In Prekmurje, Gostilna Rajh preserves the culinary heritage of the area, serving specialties like Prekmurska gibanica and dishes featuring pumpkin seed oil, a regional delicacy.

Alpine inns in the Gorenjska region serve hearty meals prepared with wild mushrooms, herbs, and fresh dairy products sourced from nearby farms. Places like Gostilna Kunstelj in Radovljica are perfect for enjoying meals with stunning views of the Julian Alps.

- Seasonal Highlights and Unique Offerings

The menus in farm-to-table restaurants and the selection at local markets change with the seasons. In spring, wild garlic, asparagus, and young lamb are in abundance. Summer brings juicy fruits like cherries and apricots, while autumn highlights mushrooms, truffles, and chestnuts. Winter is the season for preserved goods like pickles, sausages, and sauerkraut.

Honey is a staple in Slovenian markets, reflecting the country's rich beekeeping tradition. Slovenia is the birthplace of Carniolan honey bees, and honey products such as mead, propolis, and honeycomb are widely available.

Artisan cheese is another highlight, with varieties like Tolminc and Mohant offering distinct flavors tied to their regions of origin. Pair these with fresh-baked bread from local bakeries and a bottle of Slovenian wine for a true taste of the countryside.

- Interactive Experiences

Many farms and markets offer interactive experiences where visitors can participate in activities such as picking fruits, making traditional bread, or learning about cheese production. These hands-on experiences provide deeper insights into Slovenia's agricultural traditions and create lasting memories.

Local markets and farm-to-table dining in Slovenia provide a window into the country's soul, connecting visitors to its people, landscapes, and culinary heritage. Whether shopping for fresh ingredients or savoring a carefully crafted meal, these experiences are a celebration of Slovenia's deep respect for nature and tradition.

CHAPTER EIGHT

SHOPPING IN SLOVENIA

UNIQUE ARTISAN CRAFTS AND SOUVENIRS

Slovenia's artisan crafts and souvenirs are deeply rooted in the country's cultural heritage, natural landscapes, and traditional craftsmanship. Visitors to Slovenia can find unique items that reflect the skill, creativity, and spirit of its people. From intricate woodwork to hand-stitched lace, these souvenirs offer a meaningful way to take a piece of Slovenia home with you.

- Handcrafted Lace

The delicate art of lace-making is one of Slovenia's most treasured traditions, with Idrija lace being the most famous. Recognized by UNESCO as intangible cultural heritage, this intricate lace is crafted using bobbins and is known for its fine patterns. You can purchase lace doilies, tablecloths, and even jewelry at specialized shops and markets. Visiting Idrija offers a deeper experience, where you can learn about the lace-making process at the Idrija Lace School or Museum.

- Wooden Crafts

Slovenia's forests inspire beautiful wooden crafts, from decorative carvings to practical kitchenware. In the Ribnica Valley, woodworking has been a tradition for centuries, and the region is renowned for its wooden buckets, spoons, and other household items. You can find hand-carved toys, ornaments, and traditional beehive panels featuring colorful folk art motifs. Many workshops also offer demonstrations, allowing visitors to see the craftsmanship firsthand.

- Beekeeping Products

Slovenia's rich beekeeping tradition makes honey-based products a must-buy. The country is home to the Carniolan honey bee and produces high-quality honey, beeswax candles, and propolis. Traditional painted beehive panels are a unique Slovenian art form, often depicting humorous or religious scenes. These panels are both charming souvenirs and a nod to the country's deep connection to beekeeping.

- Pottery and Ceramics

Traditional Slovenian pottery reflects regional styles and practical craftsmanship. The Prekmurje region is famous for black pottery, which is both decorative and functional. Ceramic plates, mugs, and bowls with traditional motifs make excellent souvenirs. Many artisans incorporate modern designs into their work, blending tradition with contemporary aesthetics.

- Hand-Stitched Textiles

Slovenian textile art includes embroidered table linens, pillowcases, and traditional costumes. These items showcase regional patterns and techniques passed down through generations. Woolen products, such as handmade socks, scarves, and blankets, are also popular, especially in the Alpine regions where sheep farming is common.

- Glasswork and Jewelry

Slovenia has a rich history of glassmaking, particularly in regions like Rogaška Slatina. The crystal from this area is prized for its quality and craftsmanship. Visitors can find beautifully crafted wine glasses, vases, and decorative items. Slovenian jewelry often incorporates natural materials like wood, stone, and even lace patterns cast in metal, creating one-of-a-kind pieces.

- Culinary Souvenirs

For food lovers, Slovenian culinary gifts make for memorable souvenirs. Locally produced pumpkin seed oil from Prekmurje is a must-try, along with sea salt harvested from the Sečovlje Salt Pans. Dried porcini mushrooms, truffles, and herbal teas from the Alps are also popular. For spirits enthusiasts, Slivovka (plum brandy) and honey liqueurs are traditional favorites.

- Wines and Craft Beers

Slovenia's wine regions produce exceptional wines that make ideal gifts. From the crisp whites of Podravje to the bold reds of Primorska, there's a wine for every palate. Many wineries sell limited-edition bottles, perfect for a special souvenir. Slovenia's burgeoning craft beer scene also offers unique brews with local ingredients, available in specialty shops and breweries.

- Art and Prints

Local artists capture Slovenia's stunning landscapes and cultural motifs in paintings, prints, and postcards. Markets and galleries often feature these works, offering a chance to take home a piece of Slovenia's natural beauty or urban charm.

- Where to Find Slovenian Crafts

Local markets, craft fairs, and artisan workshops are the best places to find authentic Slovenian crafts. The Central Market in Ljubljana is a hub for handmade goods, while regions like Bled, Bohinj, and Ptuj are known for their boutique shops. Many artisans also open their studios to visitors, providing insights into their creative process and the stories behind their work.

Slovenia's artisan crafts and souvenirs are more than just keepsakes—they are a reflection of the country's history, traditions, and natural resources. Each item tells a story, making them a meaningful way to remember your time in this enchanting country.

SHOPPING STREETS IN LJUBLJANA AND BEYOND

Shopping in Slovenia offers a delightful mix of modern retail experiences and traditional artisanal products, with Ljubljana being the central hub of shopping activity. Whether you're looking for high-end brands, unique local crafts, or regional specialties, the country offers a wide variety of shopping streets and districts to explore.

- Ljubljana's Shopping Streets

Ljubljana, the capital city, features a variety of shopping options from elegant boutiques to traditional markets. The city's pedestrian-friendly center is perfect for leisurely strolls through charming streets lined with shops, cafés, and galleries.

Čop Street (Čopova Ulica) is one of the main shopping streets in Ljubljana. Here, you'll find a mix of international brands, department stores, and Slovenian fashion boutiques. This lively street leads to Prešeren Square, where you can browse for everything from cosmetics to clothing and accessories.

Stari Trg and Nova Trg are quaint, cobbled streets in the old town, home to several specialty shops selling unique Slovenian goods, including handmade jewelry, pottery, and local art. These streets offer a more intimate shopping experience with artisanal shops offering high-quality handcrafted products.

The Ljubljana Central Market, designed by architect Jože Plečnik, is another must-visit for anyone looking to take home local produce, handmade goods, or traditional Slovenian food products. Open-air stalls offer fresh fruits and vegetables, cheeses, cured meats, honey, and freshly baked bread, making it a vibrant destination for both food lovers and shoppers.

Pogačarjev trg, also known as Pogačar Square, is another bustling area where visitors can find a mix of local designers, artisan boutiques, and food stalls selling Slovenian specialties.

For those interested in luxury shopping, Ljubljana offers a selection of high-end international brands at Galerija Emporium. This shopping mall is located near the city center and features a range of premium fashion, accessories, and beauty products.

- Shopping Streets Beyond Ljubljana

While Ljubljana is the main shopping hub, Slovenia's other cities also offer exciting shopping opportunities that reflect the unique character of each region.

Maribor, Slovenia's second-largest city, is home to a charming pedestrianized area in its old town, featuring boutiques, craft shops, and local designer stores. Slomškov trg and Lent, the city's historic center, are popular spots for those looking for both traditional Slovenian crafts and modern fashion. Maribor is also well known for its wine culture, and you can purchase locally produced wines at various shops or directly from vineyards in the surrounding area.

In Piran, a picturesque coastal town, shopping is more focused on local artisan products and coastal-themed souvenirs. The narrow streets around Tartini Square feature shops selling high-quality local olive oils, handmade jewelry, and sea salt, as well as clothing inspired by the seaside.

In Bled, visitors can shop for local crafts, especially items related to the region's famous lake. Bled's old town offers small boutiques with handcrafted goods such as wooden products, lace, and honey-based items. A visit to Lake Bled is also an opportunity to purchase souvenirs like Bled Cream Cake and local wines from the surrounding area.

The Vipava Valley, known for its wine production, has a number of specialty wine shops and small boutique stores where visitors can buy locally produced wines and artisanal foods. The quaint village of Vipava itself offers a charming mix of wine shops and farm-to-table products.

Celje, a city with a rich history, offers a mix of modern shopping malls and quaint boutiques. The historic center, near Celje Castle, is home to shops selling everything from Slovenian clothing brands to handmade home goods.

- Specialty Shopping

Slovenia is also known for its specialty stores offering unique products that highlight the country's rich craftsmanship. Many of these can be found in towns and villages across the country. For example, the town of Idrija is famous for its Idrija lace, and visitors can purchase beautiful lace items at specialized shops or even try their hand at making their own.

For food lovers, Slovenian markets and shops offer regional products such as pumpkin seed oil from Prekmurje, Slivovka (plum brandy), Truffle oil from the Karst region, and a variety of handmade chocolates.

In Rogaška Slatina, a town famous for its crystal glass, visitors can purchase high-quality crystal products like glasses, vases, and jewelry. The Rogaška Crystal store showcases beautifully crafted pieces, some of which are hand-blown and etched with intricate designs.

Bohinj and Bled are perfect for finding locally made wool products, such as socks, scarves, and blankets, inspired by traditional Alpine life.

- Shopping Centers and Malls

While Slovenia is known for its quaint streets and local shops, modern shopping malls are also available for those seeking a more contemporary shopping experience. BTC City Ljubljana, one of the largest shopping and entertainment centers in Slovenia, offers a vast selection of international brands, electronics, home goods, and entertainment options. The complex also features a large supermarket, making it convenient for everyday shopping.

Supernova shopping malls in various cities, such as Maribor and Ljubljana, offer a range of retail stores, including fashion, home goods, and technology.

Shopping in Slovenia, whether in its bustling capital or charming smaller towns, provides a range of experiences that cater to all tastes. From designer boutiques and local fashion to artisan crafts, specialty foods, and regional products, Slovenia offers something for every shopper. Exploring the local markets, artisanal shops, and picturesque streets is an excellent way to uncover the country's culture, traditions, and creativity while bringing home a unique piece of Slovenian heritage.

LOCAL DELICACIES TO BRING HOME

Bringing home local delicacies from Slovenia is a wonderful way to preserve the memories of your trip while sharing a taste of the country with friends and family. Slovenian cuisine is rich in regional flavors, and its artisanal products are often handcrafted using traditional methods passed down through generations. Here are some of the top local delicacies to consider when shopping for souvenirs to take home.

- Slovenian Honey

Slovenia is known for its rich beekeeping tradition, with the Carniolan honey bee being a national treasure. Slovenian honey is of exceptional quality, and you can find varieties ranging from wildflower honey to chestnut and acacia honey. Many honey products, such as mead (fermented honey drink), honeycomb, and propolis, are also available in beautifully crafted jars. These make wonderful gifts for anyone who enjoys natural products and artisanal food.

- Pumpkin Seed Oil (Bučno Olje)

Hailing from the Prekmurje region in northeastern Slovenia, pumpkin seed oil is one of the country's most beloved culinary products. The oil, pressed from roasted pumpkin seeds, has a rich, nutty flavor and is used in a variety of Slovenian dishes, from salads to soups. The oil is often packaged in decorative bottles, making it an attractive and practical souvenir.

- Slovenska Potica

A true Slovenian tradition, potica is a rolled cake made with a variety of fillings, the most common being walnut, poppy seed, or tarragon. It is often served during holidays and special occasions, and taking home a beautifully wrapped potica is a great way to share a piece of Slovenian culture with others. While you can find ready-made potica in bakeries across Slovenia, it's also possible to purchase it directly from the artisans who make it in small local bakeries.

- Carniolan Sausage (Kranjska Klobasa)

The iconic Kranjska klobasa is one of Slovenia's most famous sausages, made from pork, beef, and spices. This delicacy is protected as a traditional specialty and is often enjoyed with mustard and sauerkraut. You can bring home vacuum-sealed packages of this sausage, which will last for several weeks, or purchase it from butcher shops and markets. Pair it with local beer for the ultimate Slovenian culinary gift.

- Slovenian Truffles

Slovenia's Karst region is known for its high-quality truffles, both white and black, which are used in a variety of dishes. Truffle oil, truffle salt, and truffle-infused sauces are popular products to take home. These truffle-based products are often sold in artisan shops and make an excellent gift for anyone who loves gourmet foods.

- Slovenian Wines

Slovenia is home to three major wine regions—Podravje, Primorska, and Posavje—and its wines are often produced in small, family-owned wineries. You can find a wide range of wines, from crisp whites like Sauvignon Blanc and Riesling to rich reds like Merlot and Teran. For a true Slovenian souvenir, consider bringing home a bottle of wine from a local vineyard or shop specializing in regional wines. The orange wines (wines made with extended skin contact) from the Vipava Valley are also gaining international attention.

- Slivovka (Plum Brandy)

Slivovka, or plum brandy, is a traditional Slovenian spirit, often enjoyed as a digestif. Made from fermented plums, this strong, aromatic liquor has a deep flavor and is commonly consumed during family celebrations. It is often sold in decorative bottles and can be a distinctive Slovenian souvenir. Other types of fruit brandies, such as pear or cherry brandy, are also popular in the country.

- Slovene Salt (Sečovlje Salt)

Slovenia's Sečovlje Salt Pans, located along the coast, are one of the few remaining traditional salt-making regions in Europe. The salt produced here is hand-harvested using age-old methods. Sečovlje salt is prized for its mineral-rich content and is available in various forms, such as fleur de sel and coarse salt. You can also find flavored salts, such as herb-infused or truffle salt, which make for unique and flavorful gifts.

- Slovenian Cheese

Slovenia produces a wide variety of cheeses, many of which are made with traditional methods and local milk. Tolminc is a semi-hard cheese from the Julian Alps with a rich, savory flavor, while Bovec cheese comes from the Soča Valley and is known for its creamy texture. Carniolan cheese and Kraški sir, a cheese made in the Karst region, are also great souvenirs. These cheeses are often sold in small cheese shops or farmers' markets across the country.

- Handcrafted Ceramics

Slovenian pottery, especially from the region of Prekmurje, is a popular souvenir. Handcrafted ceramic products like mugs, bowls, plates, and vases often feature traditional designs and vibrant colors. These artisanal pieces make excellent home decor items and provide a tangible piece of Slovenia's cultural heritage.

- Lace from Idrija

Idrija lace is one of the finest and most famous lacework traditions in Slovenia. This intricate lace-making art, which originated in the town of Idrija, is recognized as part of Slovenia's cultural heritage. You can buy delicate lace products, such as doilies, tablecloths, and handkerchiefs, or even lace jewelry. These items make elegant souvenirs that reflect the country's rich craftsmanship.

- Olive Oil from the Coast

The coastal regions of Slovenia, especially around Piran and Sečovlje, are home to olive groves that produce high-quality olive oil. Slovenian olive oil is renowned for its robust, fruity flavor and is often produced in small batches by local farmers. You can find beautifully packaged olive oils, along with other related products like olive paste and olive oil soaps, which are perfect for culinary enthusiasts.

- Traditional Wooden Crafts

Woodworking is a longstanding tradition in Slovenia, particularly in the Ribnica Valley. You can find unique wooden products such as spoons, carvings, cutting boards, and toys, often crafted by hand. These items are not only practical but also showcase the country's deep connection to its forests and woodcraft heritage.

Slovenia offers a wide variety of unique local delicacies and handcrafted products that make perfect souvenirs to take home. From delicious food items like honey, pumpkin seed oil, and truffles to intricate lace, ceramics, and wooden crafts, there is something for everyone. These items not only serve as delightful mementos of your time in Slovenia but also provide an opportunity to share the country's rich cultural heritage with others.

CHAPTER NINE

NIGHTLIFE AND ENTERTAINMENT

BARS AND CAFES IN LJUBLJANA

Ljubljana, Slovenia's vibrant capital, is home to an array of charming bars and cafes that reflect the city's relaxed, yet cosmopolitan atmosphere. Whether you're looking for a cozy spot to enjoy a coffee, a trendy bar to sip cocktails, or a traditional Slovenian tavern, Ljubljana has something for every taste. Here's a guide to some of the best bars and cafes in the city.

- Cafes in Ljubljana

Slovenia has a rich coffee culture, and Ljubljana's cafes are perfect for relaxing, people-watching, and savoring high-quality coffee. Many cafes also serve pastries and light snacks, creating a wonderful combination of flavors and experiences.

1. Café Central: Located in the heart of the city, Café Central is a classic Ljubljana institution. With its elegant interiors and outdoor seating along Prešeren Square, this café is perfect for enjoying a cup of coffee or tea while watching the bustle of the city. It offers a variety of coffee drinks, along with a selection of homemade cakes and pastries. The atmosphere is charming, with a blend of traditional and contemporary décor.

2. Café Ljubljana: Nestled on the banks of the Ljubljanica River, Café Ljubljana offers scenic views and a relaxed atmosphere. The café is a great place for people-watching, with comfortable seating both indoors and outdoors. They serve excellent coffee and delicious cakes, including traditional Slovenian pastries like kremna rezina (cream

cake). It's a popular spot for locals and tourists alike, especially during sunny afternoons.

3. Tozd: For those who enjoy a modern, hip vibe, Tozd offers a cozy yet trendy environment in the heart of Ljubljana. Known for its specialty coffee and laid-back atmosphere, this café has become a go-to spot for coffee enthusiasts. They serve locally roasted coffee, along with homemade cakes and savory options. The interior features eclectic décor, giving it a relaxed but cool ambiance.

4. Kavarna Union: Located inside the Grand Hotel Union, Kavarna Union is a beautiful historical café that has been a part of Ljubljana's social scene for over a century. Its elegant setting, complete with art nouveau-style interiors, is perfect for enjoying a classic coffee, whether you prefer

an espresso, cappuccino, or something more elaborate. The café is also known for its decadent cakes and traditional Slovenian pastries.

5. Café Čokl: Situated on Stari Trg in the old town, Café Čokl is a charming, family-run establishment that specializes in high-quality coffee and sweet treats. The café has a cozy, intimate vibe and is the perfect spot for enjoying a quiet moment. The friendly staff and delicious coffee make it a favorite for both locals and visitors.

6. Bars in Ljubljana: Ljubljana's bar scene is diverse, offering everything from classic taverns and craft beer bars to chic cocktail lounges and wine bars. Whether you're looking for a lively spot to socialize or a quiet corner for a drink, Ljubljana has it all.

7. Pritličje: Located near Congress Square, Pritličje is a popular bar with a relaxed and

creative atmosphere. It's an excellent spot for craft beer lovers, as the bar offers a wide selection of Slovenian craft brews. The ambiance is cozy and welcoming, with an emphasis on community and culture. The space also hosts live music events, art exhibitions, and other cultural activities.

8. Bar Flaherty's: If you're in the mood for an Irish pub experience, Flaherty's on Gornji Trg is the place to go. This classic pub offers a wide selection of international beers, whiskey, and cocktails, along with hearty pub food. The friendly atmosphere and lively crowd make it a popular choice for both locals and visitors. With its dark wood interiors and cozy seating, Flaherty's offers a great place to relax with a pint after a day of sightseeing.

9. The Cocktail Bar at Hotel Cubo: For a more upscale experience, The Cocktail Bar at

Hotel Cubo offers expertly crafted cocktails in an elegant setting. The bartenders are knowledgeable and skilled, and they can whip up both classic and innovative cocktails using high-quality spirits. The stylish décor, complete with soft lighting and comfortable seating, makes this bar ideal for a special night out.

10. Vinoteka Movia: If you're a wine enthusiast, Vinoteka Movia is a must-visit. This wine bar offers an impressive selection of Slovenian wines, especially from the famous Movia winery, known for its organic and biodynamic wines. The knowledgeable staff is always happy to recommend wines to suit your taste, and the bar's rustic yet elegant ambiance makes it a relaxing place to enjoy a glass (or two) of fine Slovenian wine.

11. Lajbah: For a more laid-back bar experience, head to Lajbah, located in the vibrant

Metelkova district, known for its alternative culture. The bar has a relaxed, bohemian atmosphere, with a focus on good drinks and creative cocktails. It's a great place to meet locals and enjoy live music or DJ sets in a unique setting.

12. Švicarija: Situated in a beautiful green area near Rožnik Hill, Švicarija offers a more tranquil setting for enjoying a drink. This bar is housed in a traditional Swiss-style chalet, surrounded by nature, making it a peaceful retreat from the city's hustle and bustle. It's an excellent choice for enjoying a cocktail or a cold beer on a sunny day while taking in the scenic views.

- Wine Bars in Ljubljana

Slovenia has a rich wine culture, and the capital city boasts a variety of wine bars where you can sample some of the country's best wines.

1. Dvorni Bar: Located inside the Slovenian National Theatre in Ljubljana, Dvorni Bar is a stylish wine bar offering an exceptional selection of Slovenian wines. The ambiance is sophisticated yet inviting, with knowledgeable staff who are eager to help you explore the diverse wine regions of Slovenia. This bar is perfect for wine lovers seeking an intimate and refined setting.

2. Movia Wine Bar: Another excellent choice for wine aficionados is Movia Wine Bar in the city center. It features an extensive list of wines from the famous Movia Winery, which is renowned for its biodynamic approach to winemaking. The modern, minimalist design of the bar creates a stylish environment where you can enjoy a glass of wine while learning more about Slovenian wine production.

Ljubljana's bars and cafes are a great way to experience the city's relaxed vibe and lively cultural scene. Whether you're sipping a perfectly brewed coffee in a charming café or enjoying a craft beer in a trendy bar, there's something to suit every taste. From historical cafés to contemporary wine bars, Ljubljana offers plenty of spots to unwind, socialize, and savor the flavors of the city.

LIVE MUSIC VENUES AND FESTIVALS

Ljubljana, Slovenia's capital, is a vibrant hub for live music, with a wide variety of venues offering everything from intimate performances to large concerts. The city's music scene reflects its rich cultural heritage and modern influences, providing plenty of opportunities for visitors to enjoy a diverse range of genres. In addition to its music venues, Ljubljana is also home to a number of exciting music festivals throughout the year, celebrating everything from classical music to electronic beats. Here's a guide to the best live music venues and festivals in Ljubljana.

- Live Music Venues in Ljubljana

1. Cvetličarna: Located just outside the city center, Cvetličarna is one of Ljubljana's most well-known live music venues. This former flower market has been transformed into a large concert hall, hosting an eclectic mix of international and local acts. The venue is particularly popular for rock, metal, and electronic performances, with a spacious main hall that can accommodate a large crowd. The atmosphere here is always lively, and it's a go-to spot for those seeking high-energy live music.

2. Kino Šiška: As one of Ljubljana's most important cultural venues, Kino Šiška is a modern music venue located in a former

cinema building. It hosts a wide range of live music events, including concerts, club nights, and festivals, with a particular focus on alternative, indie, and experimental genres. Kino Šiška has both an intimate concert hall and a larger space for bigger performances, and it's renowned for its excellent acoustics and diverse programming. Whether you're into jazz, rock, or electronic music, Kino Šiška is a must-visit for music lovers.

3. Metelkova Mesto: Metelkova Mesto is an alternative cultural center and a haven for underground music in Ljubljana. Situated in a former military barracks, Metelkova is home to a number of clubs and bars, many of which host live music events. The area is known for its punk, rock, metal, and electronic music scenes, with venues like Klub Menza Pri Koritu and Punk Rock Museum regularly hosting live performances. Metelkova is also a great place to discover

local indie artists, making it a unique destination for those looking to explore Ljubljana's alternative culture.

4. Jazz Club Ljubljana: For jazz lovers, Jazz Club Ljubljana is a must-visit venue. Located in the heart of the city, this intimate club offers regular live jazz performances, showcasing both local and international talent. The club's cozy atmosphere and excellent acoustics make it an ideal spot to enjoy a laid-back evening of smooth jazz. It's also a great place to experience some of Slovenia's top jazz musicians in a more personal setting.

5. Bistro & Bar Kljub: If you're looking for a venue that offers live music in a more relaxed setting, Kljub is a great choice. This cozy bar and bistro is known for its live acoustic performances, often featuring local singer-songwriters, folk bands, and jazz

musicians. It's a perfect spot to enjoy a casual night out with a glass of wine while listening to live tunes in a laid-back environment.

6. Channel Zero: Located in the heart of the city, Channel Zero is a popular venue for electronic music and live DJ performances. This underground club has a cutting-edge sound system and hosts regular techno, house, and drum-and-bass nights. If you're into electronic beats, Channel Zero offers a high-energy experience with top local and international DJs spinning throughout the week.

- Music Festivals in Ljubljana

1. Ljubljana Festival: One of the most prestigious cultural events in Slovenia, the Ljubljana Festival celebrates music, theater, and dance. Held annually in the summer

months, the festival brings world-class musicians and performers to Ljubljana's outdoor venues, such as the Križanke Summer Theatre and Congress Square. The festival's program includes classical music concerts, opera performances, ballet, and jazz, with performances by renowned orchestras, soloists, and conductors from around the world. For music lovers, the Ljubljana Festival is an event not to be missed.

2. Metelkova Live: Held in the alternative district of Metelkova Mesto, Metelkova Live is a festival dedicated to showcasing underground and alternative music. The event features a wide range of genres, including punk, rock, electronic, and experimental music, with performances spread across the various clubs and bars in the area. Metelkova Live is a great way to experience the alternative music scene in

Ljubljana and discover new and exciting local artists.

3. Ljubljana Jazz Festival: The Ljubljana Jazz Festival is one of the oldest jazz festivals in Europe, and it's a key event for jazz enthusiasts. Held every summer, the festival attracts some of the world's top jazz musicians, with performances taking place at various venues around the city, including Kino Šiška, Cankarjev Dom, and open-air stages. The festival covers a wide range of jazz styles, from traditional to contemporary, and it's a great way to immerse yourself in Ljubljana's jazz culture.

4. The Coke Live Festival: For fans of rock and pop music, the Coke Live Festival is a major event in Ljubljana. This festival, held every summer, features performances by top international and local bands and musicians, covering everything from rock and pop to

electronic and hip-hop. The festival's open-air setting and lively atmosphere make it a great way to experience live music in the heart of Ljubljana.

5. Druga Godba Festival: The Druga Godba Festival is an annual world music festival that celebrates diverse genres from around the globe. Held in Ljubljana and other Slovenian cities, the festival features performances by artists from Africa, Asia, Latin America, and Eastern Europe, among others. It's a great way to experience global sounds and rhythms in an exciting, multicultural atmosphere. The festival also includes workshops, screenings, and cultural events, making it a full cultural experience.

6. MetalDays: Although held just outside Ljubljana in Tolmin, MetalDays is one of the biggest heavy metal festivals in Slovenia, attracting metal fans from all over the world.

This week-long festival offers an incredible lineup of international metal bands, with performances in various subgenres, from classic metal to death and black metal. If you're visiting Ljubljana in late July, consider making the short trip to Tolmin for one of the most electrifying music festivals in the region.

7. Punk Rock Holiday: Another festival outside Ljubljana, but very popular among the city's alternative music fans, is Punk Rock Holiday in Tolmin. This punk rock festival is an annual gathering for fans of the genre, featuring live performances by top punk bands from around the world. The festival has a laid-back atmosphere and a loyal following, making it a unique music experience for visitors who love punk rock.

Ljubljana's live music scene offers a vibrant mix of venues and festivals that cater to a wide range of musical tastes. Whether you're interested in classical music, jazz, alternative rock, or electronic beats, the city's diverse offerings are sure to impress. From intimate clubs and cultural venues to large-scale music festivals, Ljubljana provides ample opportunities to enjoy live music in an unforgettable setting. Whether you're a local or a visitor, the city's music scene is an essential part of its cultural identity and a fantastic way to experience its dynamic energy.

TRADITIONAL FOLK PERFORMANCES

Traditional folk performances in Slovenia provide a captivating window into the country's rich cultural heritage, reflecting its deep connection to music, dance, and storytelling. These performances are vibrant, colorful, and rooted in centuries-old traditions passed down through generations. Whether it's folk dances performed in elaborate costumes, traditional music played on unique instruments, or folk festivals showcasing Slovenian customs, experiencing these performances is an immersive way to understand the country's identity.

- Traditional Folk Dance

Slovenian folk dance is one of the most prominent expressions of the country's culture. The dances are lively and often performed in groups, representing different regions of Slovenia. Each region has its own distinct dance style and costumes that reflect its local history, environment, and customs.

The most well-known Slovenian folk dance is the Polka, a fast-paced and rhythmic dance that often features couples spinning and stepping in time with the music. The Polka has become synonymous with Slovenian cultural identity and is frequently performed at cultural events and celebrations across the country.

Another traditional dance is the Kolo, a circle dance performed in groups, where dancers hold hands and move in unison to the beat of traditional folk music. This communal dance represents harmony and connection, often accompanied by lively accordion tunes.

The dancers typically wear traditional costumes known as narodne noše, which vary by region. Costumes are colorful and intricately designed, featuring embroidered blouses, decorative aprons, vests, and accessories such as headscarves, hats, or leather shoes called opanki. The craftsmanship of these garments is a testament to the importance of tradition and artistry in Slovenian culture.

- Traditional Folk Music

Folk music is at the heart of Slovenia's cultural identity and often accompanies folk dances and other traditional celebrations. The music features a range of instruments that produce cheerful and rhythmic melodies, evoking a sense of community and festivity.

The accordion (known as frajtonarca) is the most iconic instrument in Slovenian folk music. Its bright and vibrant sound has become a hallmark of traditional performances, particularly in rural areas and during celebrations. The accordion is often paired with instruments like the violin, double bass, clarinet, and zither (a stringed instrument called cimbale).

Slovenian folk songs tell stories of daily life, love, nature, and folklore, passed down orally through generations. Many of these songs are performed in choirs, with layered harmonies that create a rich and melodic sound. Male vocal groups, such as those performing traditional Slovenian partisan and folk songs, are particularly beloved for their deep, resonant singing style.

- Folk Festivals and Celebrations

Folk performances often take center stage at Slovenia's many festivals and celebrations, where locals and visitors alike can experience the beauty of traditional music, dance, and crafts. Some of the most notable folk festivals include:

1. Jurjevanje Festival: Held in Črnomelj, the Jurjevanje Festival is Slovenia's oldest folk festival, celebrating the arrival of spring and the country's cultural heritage. The festival features folk dance performances, live music, and displays of traditional costumes, with performers coming from across Slovenia and neighboring countries. It's a lively celebration filled with energy, where folk groups showcase the diversity of Slovenian traditions.

2. Folkart Festival: Part of the Festival Lent in Maribor, the Folkart Festival is an international celebration of folklore and tradition. It brings together folk groups from

around the world, showcasing their dances, costumes, and music alongside Slovenian performers. This festival highlights Slovenia's rich cultural heritage while fostering an appreciation for global folk traditions.

3. Kurentovanje Festival: Held in Ptuj, the Kurentovanje Festival is one of Slovenia's most famous and unique cultural celebrations. It features the traditional Kurenti, mythical creatures clad in sheepskin and adorned with bells and feathers, who perform dances to chase away winter and welcome spring. This UNESCO-recognized event combines folk music, dance, and costumes in a spectacular display of Slovenian heritage.

4. Bled Festival: The picturesque town of Bled hosts various cultural events throughout the year, often featuring traditional folk performances as part of its program. Folk

dance groups, choirs, and musicians frequently perform against the stunning backdrop of Lake Bled and Bled Castle, creating a magical atmosphere for spectators.

5. Harvest Festivals: Throughout rural Slovenia, traditional harvest festivals celebrate the end of the farming season with folk music, dancing, and food. These events are deeply rooted in the country's agricultural heritage and often feature parades of locals dressed in traditional costumes, performing folk songs and dances in gratitude for a successful harvest.

- Folk Performances in Cultural Centers and Villages

In addition to festivals, visitors can often find traditional folk performances in cultural centers, theaters, and local villages. Many smaller towns host folk groups who perform at seasonal events, weddings, and communal celebrations.

The Slovenian Ethnographic Museum in Ljubljana is an excellent place to learn about folk traditions, costumes, and instruments. It often hosts events and performances that provide insight into Slovenia's cultural heritage.

In villages, traditional performances are frequently part of religious celebrations, such as St. Martin's Day (celebrating the wine harvest) or Christmas and Easter festivals. Here, folk traditions are preserved in their most authentic form, offering visitors a genuine experience of Slovenian culture.

- Preservation of Slovenian Folk Traditions

Slovenia places a strong emphasis on preserving its folk heritage through organizations, cultural institutions, and folklore groups. Many local groups, known as folklorne skupine, are dedicated to practicing and performing traditional dances, music, and songs. These groups play a vital role in keeping Slovenia's rich traditions alive and sharing them with future generations.

Schools and cultural centers often teach children traditional dances and songs as part of their education, ensuring that folk culture remains an integral part of Slovenian life. Visitors may even have the chance to learn a few steps of a traditional dance or participate in a community folk performance, adding to the immersive experience.

Traditional folk performances are a vibrant and essential part of Slovenia's cultural identity. Whether it's through lively dances in colorful costumes, cheerful melodies played on accordions, or storytelling through song, these performances showcase the rich history and spirit of Slovenian people. Attending a folk festival, witnessing a dance performance, or exploring local celebrations offers a unique and unforgettable glimpse into Slovenia's living traditions. For visitors seeking an authentic cultural experience, Slovenian folk performances provide a captivating connection to the country's heritage.

CHAPTER TEN

DAY TRIPS AND EXCURSIONS

LAKE BOHINJ

Lake Bohinj is a serene and breathtaking natural gem located in the heart of Slovenia's Triglav National Park, the country's only national park. As the largest permanent natural lake in Slovenia, Lake Bohinj is renowned for its unspoiled beauty, crystal-clear waters, and tranquil surroundings. Surrounded by the towering peaks of the Julian Alps and dense forests, the lake is a perfect retreat for nature lovers, outdoor enthusiasts, and anyone seeking peace and relaxation away from bustling tourist hubs.

- The Beauty of Lake Bohinj

Lake Bohinj, often referred to as Slovenia's hidden paradise, lies about 26 kilometers from the more popular Lake Bled. Unlike Lake Bled's postcard-perfect fairytale charm, Lake Bohinj captivates visitors with its rugged and raw natural beauty. The lake's glassy surface reflects the surrounding mountains, creating a picture-perfect scene in every season. Whether in spring when the meadows are blooming, summer when the lake glistens under the sun, autumn when golden leaves line its shores, or winter when snow-capped peaks add a magical touch, Lake Bohinj is stunning year-round.

The lake spans approximately 4.2 kilometers in length and 1 kilometer in width, covering an area of 318 hectares. Its clear waters are fed by the Savica River, which cascades down from the nearby mountains as the iconic Savica Waterfall.

- Activities Around Lake Bohinj

Lake Bohinj is an outdoor lover's paradise, offering a variety of activities for visitors of all ages and interests.

1. Swimming and Water Sports: The lake's crystal-clear waters, which maintain a refreshing temperature in summer, make it a fantastic place for swimming, kayaking, stand-up paddleboarding (SUP), and canoeing. Boats are available for rent near the village of Ribčev Laz, and since motorized boats are not permitted, the lake retains its tranquil, pristine atmosphere.

2. Hiking and Walking: The area around Lake Bohinj offers countless hiking and walking trails suitable for all levels of fitness. A leisurely stroll around the lake takes around 3 to 4 hours and offers stunning views of the water and surrounding mountains. More adventurous hikers can embark on trails leading to nearby peaks, such as Vogel, Pršivec, or the Komna Plateau, for panoramic views of the lake and beyond. A short hike leads to the famous Savica Waterfall, one of Slovenia's most iconic

natural landmarks. The waterfall drops 78 meters in a stunning, emerald-green cascade and is considered the source of the lake. For a small entrance fee, visitors can follow a well-maintained path and steps to reach a perfect viewing spot.

3. Cycling: Cycling enthusiasts will find plenty of options around Lake Bohinj, from flat trails along the lake to more challenging mountain biking routes. E-bike rentals are available in nearby villages, making it easy for visitors to explore the lake and surrounding valleys.

4. Rowing and Fishing: Lake Bohinj is also a popular destination for fishing, with permits available for visitors who want to try their hand at catching trout, grayling, and other species. The peaceful setting makes it a great spot for a relaxing day by the water.

5. Vogel Cable Car and Ski Resort: For those looking to experience the region from above, the Vogel Cable Car provides a quick ascent to the Vogel Ski Resort. In summer, the resort serves as a fantastic hiking and viewpoint destination, offering sweeping views of Lake Bohinj and the Julian Alps. In winter, Vogel transforms into a popular ski resort with well-maintained slopes and breathtaking alpine scenery, making it ideal for skiing, snowboarding, and sledding.

6. Paragliding: Adventurers can take to the skies with paragliding over Lake Bohinj, launching from nearby hills and mountains. The bird's-eye view of the shimmering lake, lush forests, and rugged peaks is an unforgettable experience and perfect for thrill-seekers.

7. Exploring the Villages: The village of Ribčev Laz, located at the eastern end of

Lake Bohinj, serves as the gateway to the lake. Here, visitors can see the iconic Church of St. John the Baptist, a 13th-century church famous for its medieval frescoes and charming wooden bridge nearby. The peaceful village also offers cafés, restaurants, and accommodations for visitors to relax and take in the tranquil surroundings.

Nearby villages such as Stara Fužina and Bohinjska Bistrica are worth exploring for their traditional Alpine charm, wooden hayracks, and local cultural sites. Bohinjska Bistrica also features Aquapark Bohinj, a family-friendly water park with pools, saunas, and wellness areas.

- Wildlife and Nature

Lake Bohinj is part of the Triglav National Park, meaning its flora and fauna are carefully protected. The lake and its surrounding forests are home to a wide variety of wildlife, including deer, chamois, foxes, and an abundance of bird species. Birdwatchers will enjoy spotting birds such as woodpeckers, owls, and golden eagles soaring above the peaks.

The region is also known for its alpine flowers, particularly in spring and summer, when the meadows come alive with colorful blooms. Visitors can enjoy the sight of edelweiss, gentians, and wild orchids, which add to the natural beauty of the area.

- Best Time to Visit Lake Bohinj

Lake Bohinj is beautiful year-round, with each season offering something unique:

1. Spring (April to June): Wildflowers bloom, and hiking trails become accessible as the snow melts.
2. Summer (July to August): Perfect for swimming, water sports, and hiking under sunny skies.

3. Autumn (September to October): A quieter time with stunning autumn foliage and cooler weather for outdoor activities.
4. Winter (December to March): A magical snowy landscape perfect for skiing at Vogel, snowshoeing, and winter walks.

- Local Cuisine

Visitors to Lake Bohinj can savor traditional Slovenian cuisine at local restaurants and inns, known as gostilnas. Hearty dishes such as čompe s skuto (boiled potatoes with cottage cheese), jota (a sour soup with sauerkraut, beans, and sausage), and freshly-caught trout from the lake are popular choices. Don't miss tasting the regional Bohinj cheese, a semi-hard cow's milk cheese with a rich, creamy flavor, often paired with local honey and bread.

Lake Bohinj is a true natural treasure, offering a perfect blend of relaxation, adventure, and unspoiled beauty. Whether you're swimming in its clear waters, hiking through alpine trails, or simply sitting along its peaceful shores taking in the stunning views, Lake Bohinj offers an escape into nature that feels untouched and pure. Its tranquil atmosphere and diverse activities make it an unmissable destination in Slovenia for travelers seeking to reconnect with nature and experience the magic of the Julian Alps.

PIRAN AND THE SLOVENIAN COAST

Piran, a charming coastal town on Slovenia's short but stunning Adriatic coastline, is a true gem that combines Mediterranean charm, Venetian architecture, and rich cultural history. Located on the Istrian Peninsula, Piran stands out as one of the most picturesque towns in Slovenia, often referred to as the "Venetian jewel of Slovenia." Alongside neighboring coastal towns like Portorož, Izola, and Koper, Piran is part of the beautiful Slovenian Riviera, offering travelers a mix of seaside relaxation, historic exploration, and delightful cuisine.

- The Beauty and Atmosphere of Piran

Piran is a small, pedestrian-friendly town best known for its Venetian Gothic architecture, narrow cobblestone streets, and romantic atmosphere. The town stretches out onto a peninsula, surrounded by the Adriatic Sea, with breathtaking views of the turquoise waters. Its picturesque charm and historical significance make it an ideal place for visitors who enjoy both cultural exploration and seaside relaxation.

At the heart of Piran lies Tartini Square, named after the famous violinist and composer Giuseppe Tartini, who was born in Piran. The square, once a harbor, is now a vibrant open plaza surrounded by pastel-colored buildings, cafés, and landmarks, including the Tartini House, which displays memorabilia and artifacts related to Tartini's life and work. At the center of the square stands a statue of Tartini, a tribute to the town's most famous son.

The narrow alleys of Piran are perfect for wandering, leading visitors to hidden courtyards, charming shops, and small squares. The town's medieval walls and historic buildings offer stunning views of the coast and nearby towns. Sunsets over the Adriatic Sea from Piran's promenade or hilltop vantage points are a truly unforgettable experience.

- Top Sights and Landmarks in Piran
1. St. George's Church: The iconic St. George's Church dominates Piran's skyline, perched on a hill overlooking the town and the sea. Dedicated to the patron saint of Piran, the church is an excellent example of Venetian Renaissance architecture. Visitors can climb the bell tower, a replica of St. Mark's Campanile in Venice, for panoramic views of the town, the Slovenian coastline,

and even the Italian and Croatian coasts on clear days.

2. Piran Town Walls: Piran's medieval town walls date back to the 7th century and were built to protect the town from invaders. Visitors can walk along the well-preserved walls, offering spectacular views of the red-tiled rooftops, the Adriatic Sea, and the picturesque landscape beyond. The walls are particularly beautiful at sunset when the golden light highlights the town's rich colors.

3. Tartini Square and Tartini House: Tartini Square serves as the cultural and social center of Piran, surrounded by elegant buildings, including the 19th-century Town Hall and Venetian House, a stunning example of Venetian Gothic architecture. The Tartini House is a small museum showcasing the legacy of Giuseppe Tartini, including his original manuscripts,

instruments, and personal items. The square often hosts concerts, festivals, and markets, making it a lively gathering place.

4. Piran Maritime Museum: Located in the historic Gabrielli Palace, the Piran Maritime Museum tells the story of the town's maritime heritage and connection to the sea. Exhibits include models of ships, maritime tools, artifacts, and stories of Piran's seafaring past, reflecting the region's deep ties to fishing and trade.

5. The Aquarium of Piran: The Aquarium of Piran is a small but fascinating place to visit, particularly for families. It showcases the diverse marine life of the Adriatic Sea, including fish, crustaceans, and sea plants. It's an excellent way to learn about the underwater world of Slovenia's coastline.

6. Promenade and Beaches: The Piran Promenade runs along the edge of the peninsula and offers a relaxing walk with views of the calm Adriatic Sea. Visitors can find small spots to swim or sunbathe along the waterfront. While Piran itself does not have sandy beaches, the clear waters and rocky shores are ideal for swimming and snorkeling. Nearby beaches like Fiesa Beach and Bernardin Beach provide more opportunities for sunbathing and seaside activities.

- The Slovenian Coast Beyond Piran

While Piran is undoubtedly the star of Slovenia's coastline, the nearby towns of Portorož, Izola, and Koper offer additional opportunities for exploration.

1. Portorož: Just a few kilometers from Piran, Portorož is a popular resort town known for its luxury hotels, wellness spas, and vibrant

nightlife. The town's sandy beaches and thermal saltwater spas make it a popular choice for travelers seeking relaxation and entertainment.

2. Izola: The charming fishing town of Izola offers a quieter, more authentic atmosphere with its colorful old town, seafood restaurants, and marina. Izola is perfect for those who want to enjoy coastal charm without the crowds.

3. Koper: The largest town on the Slovenian coast, Koper is a mix of history and modern development. Its well-preserved medieval core features landmarks like the Praetorian Palace and Titov Trg square, while its bustling port makes it a key economic hub.

- Seafood and Cuisine on the Slovenian Coast

The cuisine in Piran and along the Slovenian coast is heavily influenced by the Mediterranean, featuring fresh seafood, olive oil, and regional wines. Local specialties include grilled sea bass, calamari, and the famous Istrian black risotto made with cuttlefish ink. The region is also known for its salt pans at nearby Sečovlje, where high-quality sea salt has been harvested for centuries. Visitors can tour the salt pans and purchase locally produced salt as a souvenir.

For dessert, try fritule, small deep-fried pastries, or Slovenian gelato, which rivals Italian versions in quality and flavor. Local wines such as Refošk and Malvazija pair perfectly with coastal dishes, offering a true taste of the Istrian region.

- Activities and Experiences

In addition to sightseeing, Piran and the surrounding coast offer plenty of activities. Visitors can enjoy boat tours, sailing trips, and snorkeling excursions to explore the Adriatic's calm, clear waters. Cycling along coastal paths is another popular activity, with scenic routes leading through vineyards, olive groves, and charming seaside towns.

The nearby Sečovlje Salina Nature Park is a must-visit for nature lovers and birdwatchers. This unique landscape features salt flats, wetlands, and diverse bird species, offering both a peaceful retreat and a fascinating look at traditional salt production.

Best Time to Visit Piran and the Slovenian Coast
The best time to visit Piran and the Slovenian coast is during the spring (April to June) and early autumn (September to October) when the weather is warm, and the crowds are smaller. Summer (July and August) is peak season, with sunny days perfect for swimming, but the town can become quite busy. Winter offers a quieter experience, with mild coastal temperatures ideal for exploring Piran's historic charm.

Piran and the Slovenian coast are enchanting destinations that blend history, culture, and natural beauty in a compact and easily accessible area. Whether you're exploring Piran's medieval streets, enjoying fresh seafood by the sea, or relaxing on the coast's serene beaches, this region offers a perfect mix of relaxation and discovery. As Slovenia's coastal jewel, Piran captures the heart with its romantic Venetian atmosphere, making it a must-visit destination for travelers seeking charm, history, and the magic of the Adriatic.

EXPLORING THE KARST REGION

The Karst Region of Slovenia is a captivating area characterized by its unique limestone landscapes, underground wonders, rolling hills, and rich cultural heritage. Known for its karstic terrain, which gave its name to similar geological formations worldwide, this region is a must-visit for travelers seeking natural beauty, adventure, and authentic Slovenian experiences. The Karst Region stretches from the Ljubljana Basin down to the Adriatic Coast, encompassing caves, cliffs, sinkholes, and charming villages.

- The Unique Karst Landscape

The Karst Region is defined by its porous limestone bedrock, which has been shaped over millions of years by water erosion, creating a fascinating underground world of caves, rivers, and tunnels. Above ground, the terrain is dotted with sinkholes, dry valleys, and rugged hills. These formations, known as karst phenomena, include famous landmarks such as caves, natural bridges, and underground rivers.

The region's limestone soil and Mediterranean climate also create ideal conditions for vineyards, olive groves, and the growth of teran, a unique red wine that thrives in this area. The Karst is also famous for its iconic stone-built architecture, including dry-stone walls and traditional karst houses.

- Top Attractions in the Karst Region
1. Postojna Cave: One of Slovenia's most famous landmarks, Postojna Cave is a spectacular 24-kilometer-long cave system formed by the Pivka River. Visitors can explore its vast underground halls, stalactites, and stalagmites on a guided tour, which includes a thrilling ride on an electric train that takes you deep into the cave. Postojna Cave is home to the olm, or "human fish," a rare and fascinating cave-dwelling amphibian.

2. Škocjan Caves: The Škocjan Caves, a UNESCO World Heritage Site, are among the most awe-inspiring natural wonders in the Karst Region. The caves feature a colossal underground canyon carved by the Reka River, along with massive chambers,

waterfalls, and impressive rock formations. Walking through the caves offers a surreal experience, with suspended bridges and dramatic views of the rushing river below. Škocjan Caves are a prime example of the Karst region's geological marvels and a must-see for nature lovers.

3. Predjama Castle: Located near Postojna Cave, Predjama Castle is a stunning medieval fortress built into the mouth of a cliffside cave. It is the largest cave castle in the world and a testament to the ingenuity of medieval architecture. Visitors can explore its hidden tunnels, chambers, and secret passageways, while the surrounding forested landscape adds to its fairy-tale atmosphere. The castle is linked to the legendary story of Erazem of Predjama, a rebellious knight who famously used the castle's secret passages to evade capture.

4. Lipica Stud Farm: The Lipica Stud Farm is the birthplace of the world-renowned Lipizzaner horses, a breed celebrated for its elegance, strength, and connection to the Spanish Riding School in Vienna. Established in 1580, Lipica is one of the oldest stud farms in Europe and offers visitors the chance to tour the stables, watch horse performances, and learn about the history of this noble breed. The serene grounds of the farm, surrounded by rolling meadows and forests, make it a perfect place for a leisurely visit.

5. Vilenica Cave: Vilenica Cave is another impressive cave system in the Karst Region, known for its beautiful stalactites, stalagmites, and underground halls. It is considered the oldest show cave in Europe, having been open to visitors since the 17th century. Vilenica's ethereal formations make

it a less crowded yet equally fascinating alternative to Postojna and Škocjan Caves.

6. Karst Villages: The Karst Region is dotted with charming villages that showcase the area's unique architecture and traditions. Villages such as Štanjel, Dutovlje, and Tomaj are known for their stone houses, narrow streets, and terraced landscapes. Štanjel, in particular, is a highlight, with its hilltop medieval center, beautiful gardens, and panoramic views of the surrounding countryside. The Ferrari Garden in Štanjel is a peaceful oasis featuring stone terraces and Mediterranean vegetation.

● Culinary Delights of the Karst Region

The Karst Region is a gastronomic paradise, offering a variety of traditional dishes and flavors that reflect its cultural heritage and natural resources.

1. Prosciutto (Pršut): The Karst Region is famous for its Karst pršut, an air-dried ham cured with the help of the region's unique microclimate and the bora wind, a dry, cold breeze that aids in the curing process. Pairing pršut with a glass of local teran wine is a classic Karst experience.

2. Teran Wine: The red soil of the Karst Region produces teran, a robust red wine made from the refošk grape. Known for its rich flavor and high iron content, teran is a perfect accompaniment to the region's hearty dishes, including meats and cheeses. Wineries across the Karst offer tastings and tours, allowing visitors to savor this local specialty.

3. Local Delicacies: Other culinary highlights include štruklji (rolled dumplings filled with cottage cheese or other ingredients), hearty stews, and dishes featuring wild asparagus, mushrooms, and herbs foraged from the

region. Visitors should also try jota, a traditional soup made with sauerkraut, beans, and pork.

- Outdoor Adventures

The Karst Region offers a variety of outdoor activities for nature lovers and adventurers.

1. Hiking and Cycling: The rolling hills, vineyards, and forested landscapes of the Karst Region are perfect for hiking and cycling. Popular trails include routes around Štanjel, the Karst Edge, and paths leading to the viewpoints of Nanos Plateau, offering sweeping vistas of the surrounding terrain.

2. Cave Exploration: In addition to show caves like Postojna and Škocjan, adventurers can explore lesser-known caves on guided tours, including diving tours in underground rivers and lakes.

3. Wildlife Watching: The Karst Region is home to a variety of flora and fauna, including rare plants, birds, and bats. Nature reserves such as the Karst Living Museum offer opportunities for visitors to learn about the region's biodiversity and ecology.

- Best Time to Visit the Karst Region

The Karst Region is a year-round destination, with each season offering something unique.

1. Spring (April to June): The landscape blooms with wildflowers, and the weather is perfect for outdoor activities.
2. Summer (July to August): Ideal for exploring caves and enjoying cooler underground temperatures.
3. Autumn (September to October): Harvest season brings wine festivals, fresh produce, and colorful vineyards.

4. Winter (November to March): Quieter months are ideal for exploring castles and villages without crowds.

The Karst Region of Slovenia is a captivating blend of natural wonders, cultural heritage, and culinary excellence. Whether exploring the awe-inspiring caves, strolling through charming stone villages, or tasting the region's renowned pršut and teran wine, visitors will find countless opportunities to connect with the landscape and traditions of this unique part of Slovenia. For travelers seeking adventure, history, and authentic local experiences, the Karst Region is a must-visit destination that showcases the true beauty of Slovenia's diverse terrain.

CROSS-BORDER TRIPS TO ITALY, AUSTRIA, OR CROATIA

Slovenia's central location in Europe makes it an excellent hub for cross-border trips to neighboring countries such as Italy, Austria, and Croatia. With efficient transportation connections, travelers can easily explore the rich history, culture, and landscapes of these nearby destinations, many of which are just a short drive, train, or bus ride away. Whether you're interested in historical cities, alpine scenery, or coastal relaxation, Slovenia offers seamless access to some of Europe's most iconic locations.

Italy is one of the closest and most popular cross-border destinations from Slovenia. The northeastern Italian regions are easily accessible, offering Mediterranean charm, rich cultural heritage, and stunning coastal towns. Trieste, a historic port city, is located just 30 minutes from the Slovenian border and makes for an ideal day trip. Known for its mix of Italian, Austrian, and Slovenian influences, Trieste is a vibrant city with grand Habsburg architecture, lively squares, and panoramic views of the Adriatic Sea. Piazza Unità d'Italia, one of Europe's largest seafront squares, and Miramare Castle, a 19th-century palace overlooking the sea, are key highlights. Trieste is also famous for its coffee culture, being home to Illy Coffee. Just a few hours further lies Venice, the magical city of canals. Visitors can explore its labyrinth of waterways, admire landmarks such as St. Mark's Square and the Rialto Bridge, or experience a gondola ride on the Grand Canal. Venice's timeless beauty and rich history make it a must-see destination. Udine, another charming Italian town close to Slovenia, is known for its Venetian architecture, cozy squares, and culinary delights. Visitors can stroll through Piazza della Libertà and enjoy Friulian cuisine in this relaxed yet culturally rich town. Along the Italian coastline, Grado offers sandy beaches, thermal spas, and a peaceful seaside atmosphere. Known as the "Sunny Island," Grado is perfect for relaxation and fresh seafood.

Austria lies just north of Slovenia and offers visitors stunning alpine landscapes, historical cities, and charming villages. Graz, Austria's second-largest city, is only two hours from Ljubljana and is a UNESCO World Heritage Site. Known for its beautifully preserved old town, Graz features Renaissance courtyards, Baroque palaces, and lively squares. Schlossberg Hill, with its panoramic views of the city, and the futuristic Kunsthaus Graz art museum are highlights for visitors. The city's culinary scene is also a delight, offering Styrian specialties and local wines. Klagenfurt, located just over an hour from Slovenia, sits on the shores of Lake Wörthersee. The town's elegant architecture, charming streets, and lakeside promenades make it a perfect destination for a relaxing day. Visitors can swim in the turquoise waters of Wörthersee or take in the beautiful alpine views. Villach, another charming Austrian town, offers medieval architecture, thermal spas, and easy access to the surrounding Carinthian Alps. The town's old center features cobbled streets and historic buildings, while the nearby mountains provide excellent hiking and skiing opportunities depending on the season. For travelers seeking a longer trip, Salzburg, the birthplace of Mozart, is a magical city approximately three to four hours from Slovenia. Salzburg's baroque architecture, Mirabell Gardens, and Hohensalzburg Fortress provide visitors with both history and beauty, surrounded by breathtaking alpine scenery.

Croatia, Slovenia's southern neighbor, offers a mix of stunning Adriatic coastlines, charming medieval towns, and natural wonders. Zagreb, the capital of Croatia, is only two hours from Ljubljana and is a vibrant city filled with history, culture, and culinary delights. Visitors can explore the Upper Town, admire its historic churches and architecture, and experience the unique exhibits of the Museum of Broken Relationships. Zagreb's bustling Dolac Market is perfect for sampling local food and produce. Along the Istrian Peninsula, the coastal town of Rovinj is a highlight with its narrow cobbled streets, colorful houses, and vibrant harbor. Known for its picturesque old town and stunning sunsets, Rovinj offers fresh seafood, hidden beaches, and delicious local specialties such as truffles and olive oil. Pula, located nearby, is famous for its well-preserved Roman amphitheater, one of the largest in the world. Visitors to Pula can explore its ancient ruins, relax on beautiful beaches, and enjoy the relaxed coastal atmosphere. For those seeking natural beauty, Plitvice Lakes National Park is a must-visit. Located about 2.5 hours from Slovenia, Plitvice is a UNESCO World Heritage Site known for its cascading lakes, crystal-clear waterfalls, and lush forests. Visitors can wander along wooden boardwalks and take in the serene, turquoise waters that define the park. Another popular coastal destination is Opatija, often referred to as the "Austrian Riviera." This elegant town features grand villas, seaside promenades, and a calm atmosphere ideal for relaxation.

Traveling between Slovenia and its neighboring countries is made easy by well-developed transportation networks. For visitors choosing to drive, the roads are in excellent condition, and most border crossings are quick and straightforward. It is important to purchase road vignettes or toll stickers for Slovenia and neighboring countries before driving. Train travel is another convenient option, with regular routes from Ljubljana to Trieste, Graz, and Zagreb, as well as direct connections to Venice and Vienna. Buses are an affordable and reliable way to explore cross-border destinations, with international routes to major cities like Trieste, Pula, and Graz. For those seeking a stress-free experience, organized day tours are widely available, offering transportation, guided visits, and curated itineraries to popular destinations such as Postojna Cave and Pula or the Plitvice Lakes.

Slovenia's position at the crossroads of Central Europe and the Mediterranean makes it an ideal base for exploring nearby Italy, Austria, and Croatia. Whether visiting Trieste's historic squares, taking in the serene beauty of Austria's alpine lakes, or relaxing along Croatia's Adriatic coast, each destination offers something unique. These cross-border trips provide travelers with the opportunity to experience the rich culture, history, and natural beauty of Europe while making the most of Slovenia's central location.

CHAPTER ELEVEN

PRACTICAL TIPS FOR TRAVELERS

HEALTH AND SAFETY IN SLOVENIA

Slovenia is considered one of the safest and most welcoming destinations in Europe, offering travelers peace of mind while exploring its stunning landscapes, cities, and countryside. Known for its clean environment, high safety standards, and excellent healthcare system, Slovenia ensures a comfortable and worry-free travel experience. However, it is always important to stay informed and take necessary precautions to maintain health and safety throughout your trip.

Slovenia has a low crime rate, making it a very safe country for tourists, including solo travelers and families. Violent crime is extremely rare, and petty crimes like pickpocketing or scams are minimal compared to other European destinations. That being said, travelers should still exercise general caution, particularly in crowded areas such as markets, train stations, and popular tourist attractions, where petty theft can occasionally occur. It's always advisable to keep your belongings secure, carry copies of your travel documents, and avoid displaying expensive items like jewelry or electronics.

Healthcare in Slovenia is of a high standard, with modern medical facilities, well-trained healthcare professionals, and reliable emergency services. If you are a European Union (EU) citizen, the European Health Insurance Card (EHIC) grants you access to Slovenia's public healthcare system at reduced or no cost. Travelers from outside the EU are encouraged to purchase comprehensive travel insurance that covers medical care, emergency evacuation, and unexpected costs.

Pharmacies are widely available across the country, and pharmacists can provide advice or over-the-counter medications for minor ailments. Pharmacies are generally open during regular business hours, with 24-hour pharmacies available in larger cities such as Ljubljana and Maribor.

Vaccinations are not mandatory for travel to Slovenia, but it's recommended that routine vaccinations, such as tetanus, measles, mumps, rubella (MMR), and hepatitis A, are up to date before traveling. Tick-borne encephalitis (TBE) is present in some forested areas, particularly in the spring and summer months when ticks are most active. Travelers planning outdoor activities such as hiking, camping, or cycling in rural or forested regions should consider taking precautions. These include wearing long-sleeved clothing, using insect repellents with DEET, and checking for ticks after spending time outdoors. Vaccination against tick-borne encephalitis is also available and recommended for those engaging in extensive outdoor activities.

Tap water in Slovenia is of exceptional quality and is safe to drink throughout the country. Slovenia is proud of its pristine water sources, and travelers can confidently fill up reusable bottles from taps, fountains, or natural springs. The country's commitment to sustainability and environmental preservation means that water quality standards are high, making it both safe and eco-friendly to avoid bottled water.

When participating in outdoor activities, it is essential to stay aware of weather conditions and terrain. Slovenia's natural beauty, including its mountains, rivers, and caves, attracts hikers, cyclists, and adventurers. In the Julian Alps, Triglav National Park, or other mountainous areas, weather can change rapidly, so it's important to dress in layers, bring waterproof gear, and check weather forecasts before venturing out. Hikers should stick to marked trails, inform someone about their plans, and carry essentials like maps, water, and first aid kits. For more challenging hikes or activities such as mountaineering, hiring a local guide or joining organized tours is highly recommended for safety. During winter, Slovenia's ski resorts are popular, but proper safety equipment and attention to slope rules are essential to avoid accidents.

Slovenia's roads are generally safe and well-maintained, making it an excellent destination for road trips. Drivers should adhere to traffic laws, including wearing seatbelts, using headlights during the day, and maintaining speed limits. Driving under the influence of alcohol is strictly prohibited, with low legal limits. In winter, snow chains or winter tires are required in certain regions, particularly in mountainous areas. Emergency roadside assistance is available through the Slovenian Automobile Association (AMZS) for any travel disruptions.

In terms of natural safety, travelers should take care in certain environments. Slovenia's caves, such as Postojna Cave and Škocjan Caves, are incredible natural wonders, but visitors should follow safety instructions and only explore with authorized guides. Rivers, including the Soča and Sava, are popular for rafting, kayaking, and swimming, but strong currents and sudden water level changes can pose risks. When participating in water sports, ensure you are accompanied by licensed instructors and wear appropriate safety gear.

Emergency services in Slovenia are reliable and quick to respond. The European emergency number 112 can be dialed for any situation requiring medical, fire, or rescue assistance. For police services, travelers can dial 113. English-speaking operators are generally available, especially in tourist areas and major cities. Hospitals and clinics in Slovenia are well-equipped to handle emergencies, with larger cities offering specialized care.

Slovenia's well-organized infrastructure, clean environment, and strong commitment to safety ensure that visitors can relax and enjoy their time in the country. By staying aware of your surroundings, taking necessary health precautions, and following safety guidelines during outdoor activities, you can make the most of your Slovenian adventure with peace of mind. Whether you're exploring caves, hiking alpine trails, or wandering through charming cities, Slovenia is a safe and healthy destination ready to welcome travelers in 2025.

BUDGETING AND CURRENCY TIPS

Slovenia offers excellent value for travelers, making it an accessible destination for a range of budgets while still providing high-quality experiences. With proper planning and smart spending, visitors can enjoy its stunning natural beauty, charming cities, and cultural sites without overspending. Understanding the local currency, costs, and money-saving tips will help you make the most of your trip to Slovenia in 2025.

Slovenia uses the euro (EUR) as its official currency, which is convenient for travelers coming from other Eurozone countries. Banknotes are available in denominations ranging from €5 to €500, while coins come in values from 1 cent to €2. Credit cards, including Visa and Mastercard, are widely accepted in hotels, restaurants, shops, and larger attractions, especially in cities like Ljubljana, Bled, and Maribor. However, it's always a good idea to carry some cash, particularly when visiting rural areas, local markets, or smaller establishments where card payments may not be accepted. ATMs are widely available throughout the country, and withdrawing euros is easy for most international cards, though it's advisable to check with your bank regarding withdrawal fees.

Slovenia is a budget-friendly destination compared to its western European neighbors, offering affordable accommodation, food, and activities. Daily costs will vary depending on your travel style. Budget travelers can expect to spend around €50–€70 per day, covering hostel accommodations, meals at local eateries, and public transport. Mid-range travelers should budget around €100–€150 per day, which allows for comfortable hotels, sit-down meals, and entry to attractions. Luxury travelers can enjoy Slovenia's upscale hotels, fine dining, and private tours for approximately €200 or more per day.

Accommodation costs in Slovenia cater to all budgets. Hostels and budget-friendly guesthouses are available in major cities and tourist hubs, often costing between €20–€40 per night for dorm-style rooms or private rooms in basic guesthouses. Mid-range hotels, B&Bs, and boutique accommodations typically range from €60–€120 per night, offering comfort and excellent value. Luxury hotels, resorts, and wellness retreats, especially those near Lake Bled or in Ljubljana, can range from €150–€300 per night, depending on the season and amenities offered. Farm stays, a unique and affordable option, allow travelers to enjoy Slovenian hospitality in rural settings for around €40–€70 per night, often with meals included.

Dining in Slovenia is another area where you can balance quality and cost. For budget travelers, local bakeries, cafes, and street food stalls offer inexpensive meals for as little as €5–€8. Try burek, a savory pastry, or čevapčiči, grilled meat sausages, for a filling and affordable option. Mid-range restaurants serve traditional Slovenian dishes and international cuisine for around €10–€20 per meal, including hearty stews, fresh seafood, and locally sourced vegetables. Fine dining experiences in upscale restaurants or Michelin-starred establishments can cost €50 or more per person, offering gourmet dishes and excellent wine pairings. To save money, consider opting for the "kosilo", a fixed-price lunch menu offered by many restaurants, typically costing around €8–€12 and including soup, a main dish, and a salad.

Transportation in Slovenia is both efficient and affordable. Public transport, including buses and trains, connects major cities and regions at reasonable prices. A bus or train ticket between Ljubljana and popular destinations like Lake Bled or Maribor costs around €5–€10. Renting a car is a great option for exploring Slovenia's countryside, caves, and national parks, with prices starting at €30–€50 per day, depending on the vehicle and season. Fuel prices are similar to those in the rest of Europe, and tolls for using highways can be covered with a vignette, a mandatory sticker costing €15 for a week or €30 for a month.

Activities and attractions in Slovenia also offer excellent value. Many natural attractions, such as hiking trails in Triglav National Park or Lake Bohinj, are free to visit. Entrance fees for popular sites like Bled Castle, Postojna Cave, or Škocjan Caves typically range between €10–€30, depending on the location and guided tour options. To save on attractions, consider purchasing combination tickets or city cards, like the Ljubljana Card, which includes entry to major sights, public transportation, and discounts on tours.

For budget-conscious travelers, Slovenia's markets and local grocery stores offer a great way to save money on meals and snacks. Supermarkets such as Mercator, Spar, and Hofer provide affordable groceries, with fresh bread, cheese, cured meats, and fruits available for picnic-style meals. Local farmers' markets, like the one in Ljubljana's central square, are not only budget-friendly but also a great opportunity to sample Slovenian produce and traditional snacks.

Money-saving tips include traveling during the shoulder seasons of spring (April to June) and fall (September to October), when accommodation prices are lower, and crowds are smaller. Booking accommodations and tours in advance can also lead to better deals. Taking advantage of Slovenia's natural beauty, such as free hiking trails, lakes, and coastal walks, allows travelers to experience the country's highlights without added expenses.

By planning carefully, understanding the costs, and taking advantage of local offerings, you can enjoy Slovenia's rich culture, delicious cuisine, and beautiful landscapes on any budget. Whether you're staying in a luxury resort by Lake Bled, savoring budget-friendly street food in Ljubljana, or hiking through Triglav National Park for free, Slovenia promises an affordable and unforgettable travel experience.

WEATHER AND PACKING ADVICE

Slovenia experiences a diverse climate, offering something for every traveler, from warm Mediterranean summers to snowy Alpine winters. Knowing the weather patterns will help you pack appropriately and enjoy your trip no matter the season. Slovenia's geography—ranging from the Julian Alps to its Adriatic coastline—creates regional variations in temperature and weather, so it's important to plan for both outdoor activities and city exploration.

In spring (March to May), Slovenia emerges from its winter chill with milder temperatures and blooming landscapes. Average daytime temperatures range from 10°C to 20°C (50°F to 68°F). This is an excellent season for hiking, cycling, and sightseeing, as the countryside turns lush and green. Pack light layers such as long-sleeve shirts, sweaters, and a light jacket for cooler mornings and evenings. Waterproof clothing and a compact umbrella are essential, as spring can bring occasional showers. Comfortable walking shoes or hiking boots are recommended if you plan to explore rural trails or city streets.

Summer (June to August) brings warm and sunny weather across most of Slovenia, making it the peak season for tourists. Average temperatures range from 25°C to 30°C (77°F to 86°F), although it can get hotter in the lowlands and along the coast. The Adriatic Sea, Lake Bled, and Lake Bohinj become popular spots for swimming and water activities, while the Alpine regions offer cooler escapes. Pack light, breathable clothing like shorts, T-shirts, dresses, and a wide-brimmed hat to protect against the sun. Sunglasses, sunscreen, and a reusable water bottle are essential for staying hydrated and safe. For outdoor enthusiasts, sturdy shoes for hiking and quick-dry sportswear are ideal for exploring Triglav National Park or the Soča Valley. If visiting religious or historical sites, bring a lightweight scarf or shawl to cover shoulders, as modest dress is sometimes required. Even in summer, pack a light sweater or jacket for evenings, especially in the Alps, where temperatures drop.

During autumn (September to November), Slovenia transitions to cooler weather with vibrant fall foliage, particularly in the forests and mountains. Temperatures range between 10°C and 20°C (50°F to 68°F) in September and drop closer to 5°C (41°F) by November. This season is perfect for wine-tasting tours, hiking through colorful landscapes, and exploring quieter cities. Pack layers such as long-sleeve shirts, sweaters, and a waterproof jacket for unpredictable weather. A pair of sturdy shoes or boots will keep you comfortable during city walks and countryside explorations. For cooler evenings, a scarf, gloves, and a hat might be helpful, especially later in the season.

Winter (December to February) transforms Slovenia into a winter wonderland, particularly in the Alpine regions. Temperatures can range from 0°C to -5°C (32°F to 23°F) in the mountains, while coastal areas and lowlands stay milder, averaging 5°C to 10°C (41°F to 50°F). Snowfall is common in the Julian Alps, creating perfect conditions for skiing, snowboarding, and other winter sports in resorts like Kranjska Gora and Vogel. Pack thermal layers, a warm winter coat, gloves, a hat, and a scarf to stay comfortable in the cold. Waterproof and insulated boots are essential for walking in snow or slushy conditions. If you're visiting cities like Ljubljana or Maribor during winter, the festive Christmas markets create a cozy atmosphere, but you'll still want warm layers and waterproof outerwear.

No matter the season, Slovenia's weather can change quickly, especially in the mountains. If you plan to hike or explore higher altitudes, always pack layers, including a waterproof and windproof jacket. Even in summer, temperatures in the Alps can drop unexpectedly, so carrying a fleece or sweater is wise. For all seasons, a sturdy pair of walking shoes or boots will ensure comfort while exploring cities, castles, caves, or nature trails.

For travelers visiting Slovenia's diverse regions, pack according to your planned activities. If you're heading to the coast or lakes, swimwear, sandals, and sun protection are must-haves during warmer months. For activities like caving at Postojna or Škocjan, a light jacket and closed-toe shoes are necessary, as cave temperatures stay around 8°C to 10°C (46°F to 50°F) year-round. If you're visiting Slovenia for skiing or winter sports, bring appropriate gear, such as thermal wear, ski jackets, and goggles.

Equipment can also be rented at most major resorts if you prefer to travel light.

Finally, Slovenia's commitment to eco-friendly travel makes a reusable water bottle, cloth bags for shopping, and eco-friendly toiletries excellent additions to your packing list. By preparing for Slovenia's seasonal weather and packing versatile layers, you'll be ready to explore its diverse landscapes and cultural gems in comfort and style.

ESSENTIAL APPS AND TRAVEL RESOURCES

Having the right apps and resources can make your trip to Slovenia smoother, more enjoyable, and stress-free. Whether you're navigating cities, exploring rural areas, or planning activities, technology can help you find reliable information, save money, and stay connected. Here are some essential apps and travel resources to consider for your visit to Slovenia in 2025.

For Navigation and Transportation, apps like Google Maps and Waze are invaluable for getting around Slovenia by car, bike, or on foot. Google Maps provides detailed directions, public transportation schedules, and walking routes for cities like Ljubljana, Maribor, and Bled, as well as rural areas. If you're driving, Waze can help you avoid traffic and road closures, especially in peak travel seasons. For public transport, the Nomago app provides bus timetables and booking services for regional travel, while Slovenian Railways (SŽ) has its own app for train schedules and ticket purchases across the country.

For travel planning and booking, apps like Booking.com and Airbnb offer a wide range of accommodation options, from budget hostels and farm stays to luxury hotels and private apartments. Slovenia's tourism infrastructure is excellent, and booking through these platforms allows you to compare prices, read reviews, and find places that match your budget and preferences. If you're looking for last-minute deals, HotelTonight may offer discounts on spontaneous stays. For organized tours and activities, GetYourGuide and Viator provide booking options for guided tours to attractions like Postojna Cave, Bled Castle, or Soča Valley adventures.

For language and communication, Slovenia's official language is Slovenian, but English is widely spoken, especially in tourist areas. However, having a translation app like Google Translate is still useful for communicating in smaller towns, reading signs, or understanding menus in local restaurants. Download the Slovenian language pack for offline use before your trip. Another handy app is Duolingo, which can help you learn basic Slovenian phrases to enhance your experience and connect with locals.

For exploring attractions and landmarks, TripAdvisor and Google Reviews provide traveler reviews, tips, and recommendations for Slovenia's top sights, restaurants, and activities. Whether you're visiting Lake Bled, Ljubljana's Old Town, or the Škocjan Caves, these platforms help you prioritize must-see attractions and uncover hidden gems. The official Visit Slovenia app is also a great resource, offering detailed guides, travel itineraries, and updated information on events, festivals, and attractions throughout the country.

For hiking, cycling, and outdoor adventures, Slovenia is a paradise for nature lovers, and having the right tools will make exploring its landscapes easier. The Komoot app is excellent for planning hiking and cycling routes with detailed maps, trail difficulty ratings, and offline functionality. Another popular option is AllTrails, which features user-generated reviews, trail maps, and tips for hiking routes in places like Triglav National Park, the Julian Alps, and Soča Valley. For more specific outdoor exploration, Slovenian Mountain Trails is a locally-focused app with routes, hut information, and weather updates for mountain adventures.

For weather forecasts, staying updated on Slovenia's weather conditions is crucial, particularly if you plan to hike, ski, or explore caves. Apps like AccuWeather and Meteo.si (Slovenia's official weather service) provide accurate, real-time forecasts for cities, mountains, and the countryside. The Meteo.si app also includes weather warnings and radar maps, making it a reliable resource for outdoor planning.

For currency exchange and budgeting, Slovenia uses the euro (EUR), and most payments are cashless. However, it's helpful to have a currency conversion app like XE Currency or Currency Converter Plus to monitor rates and convert prices for better budgeting. Apps like Trail Wallet or Splitwise help you track expenses and split costs with travel companions.

For dining and food recommendations, Google Maps and TripAdvisor offer reviews of Slovenian restaurants, cafes, and food markets. If you want a curated selection of dining options, the Michelin Guide app lists the best restaurants across Slovenia, including those with Michelin stars or Bib Gourmand ratings. For reservations, especially in fine dining establishments, apps like TheFork allow you to book tables easily. Slovenia's food scene is diverse, and these tools will help you discover local delicacies like potica, štruklji, and fresh seafood along the coast.

For emergencies and safety, it's essential to know Slovenia's emergency numbers, including 112 for general emergencies and 113 for police assistance. The Red Cross First Aid app is a great resource to have on hand, offering quick tips and instructions in case of a medical emergency. To stay informed, download the Visit Slovenia app or check Slovenia's official tourism websites, as they often provide safety updates, contact information, and traveler advisories.

For staying connected, most travelers rely on mobile data to access apps, maps, and resources. Slovenia offers excellent mobile coverage, and eSIM apps like Airalo allow you to purchase affordable local data plans without needing a physical SIM card. Free Wi-Fi is available in most hotels, cafes, and public spaces, but downloading offline maps and resources in advance ensures you'll have access even without internet.

By using these essential apps and resources, you can simplify your travel planning, navigate Slovenia with ease, and make the most of your experience in this beautiful and diverse country. Whether you're exploring nature trails, tasting local cuisine, or discovering cultural landmarks, these tools will ensure a smooth and stress-free trip.

CHAPTER TWELVE

SLOVENIA IN 2025

UPCOMING FESTIVALS AND EVENTS

Slovenia is known for its vibrant cultural calendar, offering a mix of traditional festivals, music events, art exhibitions, and outdoor celebrations. Whether you're a fan of classical music, folk traditions, or contemporary arts, there's always something exciting happening across the country. Here are some of the upcoming festivals and events you can look forward to in Slovenia in 2025.

- Ljubljana Festival

One of the most significant cultural events in Slovenia, the Ljubljana Festival takes place every summer, usually from June to September. It features a variety of performances, including opera, ballet, classical music concerts, and theatre productions. The festival attracts world-renowned artists and offers performances at iconic venues like the Ljubljana Castle, Križanke Summer Theatre, and Congress Square. It's a must-attend for those seeking a taste of Slovenia's rich cultural heritage.

- Piran Music Festival

Held annually in the coastal town of Piran, the Piran Music Festival celebrates classical music in one of Slovenia's most picturesque settings. Set against the backdrop of the Adriatic Sea, the festival brings together musicians and music lovers for a series of concerts, often held in historical venues like the Piran Town Hall and the St. George's Church. This festival is perfect for classical music enthusiasts and those looking to enjoy Slovenia's stunning coastline.

- Bled Festival

Held in the summer, the Bled Festival is a celebration of classical music, opera, and ballet. Located in one of Slovenia's most famous tourist destinations, Lake Bled, the festival offers performances in a stunning natural setting. Concerts take place in Bled Castle, along the shores of the lake, and in the nearby Church of St. Martin. The festival is a highlight for music lovers visiting the area during the summer months.

- Kurentovanje

Held in the town of Ptuj, Kurentovanje is Slovenia's largest and most famous Carnival celebration, typically taking place in late February or early March. This vibrant, multi-day event features traditional costumes, music, dancing, and street parades, with participants wearing elaborate masks, the most iconic being the Kurent mask, a figure symbolizing the expulsion of winter. It's a lively and unique cultural experience, offering a chance to witness ancient Slovenian traditions in full swing.

- Slovenian Wine Harvest Festivals

The Slovenian Wine Harvest Festivals take place in the autumn months (September to October) and are celebrated across Slovenia's wine regions, including Maribor, Vipava Valley, and the Ptuj area. The festivals are a fantastic way to experience Slovenia's rich wine culture, with wine tastings, food pairings, and live music. The harvest season is an excellent time to visit, as you can witness local grape-picking traditions and sample wines directly from the producers.

- Festival of Ljubljana (Jazz & World Music)

In addition to the main Ljubljana Festival, the Festival of Ljubljana also hosts a series of jazz and world music performances, especially in the summer months. These events bring international artists to Slovenia, with performances held in open-air venues such as Tivoli Park, as well as intimate concert halls. Jazz lovers and fans of global rhythms will find plenty to enjoy at this lively and diverse music festival.

- International Theatre Festival

Held annually in Ljubljana, the International Theatre Festival is one of the most important cultural events in the country. It brings together theater companies from all over the world to perform on Slovenian stages. This festival typically takes place in May and features a wide variety of theatrical performances, from experimental and avant-garde productions to classical plays and contemporary pieces. It's a great opportunity for those interested in the performing arts to explore international theatre in Slovenia.

- Slovenian Festival of Music

The Slovenian Festival of Music is a celebration of traditional and modern Slovenian music, featuring performances by local and international musicians. Held in various cities across the country, including Ljubljana, Maribor, and Celje, the festival typically occurs in the late spring or summer months. The festival includes performances in genres such as classical, jazz, folk, and contemporary music, reflecting Slovenia's rich musical diversity.

- Maribor Theatre Festival

Held in Slovenia's second-largest city, Maribor, this festival is dedicated to theatre productions and takes place in late October and early November. The Maribor Theatre Festival showcases a wide range of performances, from traditional plays to innovative experimental theatre. It's a great event for theatre enthusiasts looking to experience Slovenia's cultural scene beyond its well-known music and arts festivals.

- Ljubljana Fashion Week

Fashion lovers will want to attend Ljubljana Fashion Week, held every spring and autumn in the capital. The event showcases the work of Slovenian designers and highlights global fashion trends. It features runway shows, designer exhibitions, and plenty of opportunities to see the latest in fashion, making it a must-attend for anyone with an interest in style and design.

- The Cherry Festival in Koper

Held in June, the Cherry Festival in the coastal town of Koper celebrates Slovenia's cherry-growing heritage. This vibrant festival includes a variety of activities such as fruit picking, cherry-themed culinary events, and a lively parade. It's an excellent event for foodies and families who want to experience the local culture while enjoying the beautiful Mediterranean climate.

- Truffle Festival in the Karst Region

For food lovers, the Truffle Festival in Slovenia's Karst region is a unique culinary event that takes place every autumn. The festival celebrates the region's renowned truffle production, offering guests the chance to enjoy truffle-themed dishes, wine pairings, and truffle hunting excursions. It's a fantastic opportunity to taste some of Slovenia's finest ingredients and explore the stunning Karst landscapes.

Slovenia's cultural calendar is packed with diverse and exciting events, making it an ideal destination for travelers who enjoy immersing themselves in local traditions, music, arts, and food. Whether you're visiting during the summer festival season or during the winter carnival period, there is always something happening to make your trip memorable.

ECO-TOURISM AND SUSTAINABILITY INITIATIVES

Slovenia is a leader in eco-tourism and sustainability, offering travelers a chance to explore its natural beauty while contributing to the preservation of its diverse ecosystems. The country has been recognized as a green destination, and it places great emphasis on sustainable practices in tourism, nature conservation, and local community development. If you're looking to have an environmentally responsible and enriching experience, Slovenia is an ideal destination. Here are some of the key eco-tourism and sustainability initiatives you can explore when visiting Slovenia.

- Green Destinations and Eco-Friendly Accommodation

Slovenia has made significant strides in promoting sustainable travel through the Green Scheme of Slovenian Tourism (GST). This initiative certifies destinations, attractions, and accommodations that adhere to sustainable practices, ensuring that your stay supports eco-friendly tourism. Ljubljana, the country's capital, was named a Green Capital of Europe in 2016, and it's a perfect example of a city committed to sustainability. It boasts car-free areas, extensive green spaces, and initiatives to reduce waste and energy consumption. Many hotels in Ljubljana and beyond have earned sustainability certifications like Green Key and Eco-Label, offering energy-efficient rooms, waste management programs, and locally sourced food.

For travelers looking for a more immersive eco-tourism experience, there are also options for staying in rural farm stays and eco-resorts, where local farming practices are used to promote environmental sustainability. These accommodations emphasize organic farming, conservation of water and energy resources, and waste recycling. Eco-lodges in places like Triglav National Park, Lake Bohinj, and the Soča Valley provide guests with an opportunity to experience Slovenia's nature while supporting green practices.

- Sustainable Transportation

Slovenia encourages the use of public transportation as an eco-friendly option for getting around. The country's well-connected bus and train services, especially between major cities and towns, are reliable and environmentally conscious. Ljubljana's public transport system is also car-free in certain areas, promoting walking and cycling. Slovenia's extensive cycling network, especially in the Karst region and the Soča Valley, offers travelers an opportunity to explore nature while reducing their carbon footprint. For those looking to explore the countryside or take longer road trips, renting a hybrid or electric car is another sustainable travel option. The country also has a growing number of electric vehicle (EV) charging stations, making it easier for eco-conscious visitors to travel with minimal environmental impact.

- Outdoor Activities with Minimal Environmental Impact

Slovenia's natural beauty is a major draw, and there are countless eco-friendly activities that allow visitors to explore its stunning landscapes responsibly. Hiking and cycling are popular ways to experience the country's mountains, lakes, forests, and valleys without harming the environment. Triglav National Park, the country's first and largest protected area, offers numerous eco-friendly trails that allow visitors to immerse themselves in Slovenia's pristine nature. For those interested in adventure tourism, activities like kayaking on the Soča River, caving in the Škocjan Caves, and skiing in Kranjska Gora are available with an emphasis on sustainable practices. These activities often include eco-conscious operators who ensure minimal environmental impact while preserving the natural surroundings.

- Sustainable Food Practices

Slovenia's food culture is deeply connected to the land, and sustainable farming practices are at the core of its culinary identity. Farm-to-table dining is prevalent across the country, with many restaurants and markets sourcing ingredients from local farms that prioritize organic and sustainable agriculture. The Ljubljana Central Market and smaller regional markets in towns like Maribor and Piran are excellent places to sample fresh, seasonal produce, artisan cheeses, and meats produced in harmony with the environment. Slovenia also boasts numerous vineyards that follow sustainable practices, offering wine-tasting tours with a focus on eco-friendly production methods.

- Wildlife and Nature Conservation

Slovenia is home to diverse wildlife, including bears, wolves, and lynxes, and it places a strong emphasis on conservation efforts. The country has established numerous protected areas, including nature reserves, national parks, and wetlands, to safeguard its rich biodiversity. Visitors can engage in responsible wildlife watching, whether it's spotting birds in the Sečovlje Salt Pans or observing large carnivores in the forests of the Kočevsko region. Several organizations, such as the Slovenian Forest Service, work to preserve Slovenia's wildlife and promote sustainable tourism practices.

- Eco-Friendly Festivals and Events

Slovenia's commitment to sustainability extends to its festivals and events, many of which focus on environmental awareness and eco-conscious practices. Events like the Eco Ljubljana festival celebrate sustainable living through workshops, markets, and performances that encourage recycling, renewable energy use, and environmental education. The Slow Food Festival held in various towns across Slovenia celebrates local, sustainable cuisine with an emphasis on seasonality and organic farming. For nature lovers, nature-oriented festivals such as the Triglav Festival emphasize outdoor activities that promote conservation and environmental stewardship.

- Sustainable Souvenirs

When shopping for souvenirs in Slovenia, you'll find a growing emphasis on eco-friendly products. Many local artisans create handmade goods from natural, recycled, or upcycled materials, making them both unique and sustainable. You can find locally crafted ceramics, wooden items, and textiles in craft markets and boutiques, as well as eco-conscious beauty products made with organic ingredients. These locally made souvenirs not only support the community but also reduce the carbon footprint associated with mass-produced goods.

- Responsible Waste Management

Slovenia is a pioneer in waste management and recycling, and the country has an excellent system in place for waste separation. Public spaces, hotels, and restaurants encourage waste sorting into paper, plastic, glass, and organic waste. Travelers are encouraged to do the same in order to contribute to Slovenia's recycling initiatives. Many eco-resorts and accommodations provide zero-waste amenities, including reusable water bottles, composting, and sustainable packaging.

- Eco-Tourism Certification

The Green Key and Green Globe certifications are widely recognized in Slovenia, offering travelers a guide to finding sustainable accommodation and services. The Green Scheme of Slovenian Tourism allows visitors to identify destinations and services that prioritize environmental conservation, energy efficiency, and the use of local resources.

By embracing Slovenia's eco-tourism and sustainability initiatives, you can enjoy the country's natural beauty while contributing to its efforts to protect the environment for future generations. Whether you're hiking through protected forests, enjoying farm-to-table meals, or staying in eco-certified hotels, there are plenty of ways to explore Slovenia in an environmentally responsible way.

HIDDEN GEMS AND EMERGING DESTINATIONS

Slovenia is a country known for its breathtaking landscapes and rich cultural heritage, but beyond the well-known attractions like Lake Bled and Ljubljana, there are numerous hidden gems and emerging destinations that offer a more intimate and off-the-beaten-path experience. These lesser-known places allow you to explore the quieter, more authentic side of Slovenia, where you can enjoy nature, culture, and history without the crowds. Here are some of the best hidden gems and emerging destinations in Slovenia.

- The Soča Valley

While the Soča Valley has gained popularity in recent years, it remains one of Slovenia's best-kept secrets. Known for its emerald-green river, the valley is a paradise for outdoor enthusiasts. The Soča River is perfect for kayaking, rafting, and fishing, while the surrounding mountains provide excellent hiking and mountain biking opportunities. The small towns of Kobarid, Bovec, and Tolmin offer a charming mix of history, natural beauty, and local culture. A visit to Kobarid's World War I Museum is a must, as the area played a significant role in the historical battles of the Isonzo Front.

- Škofja Loka

A picturesque medieval town, Škofja Loka is often overlooked by tourists, making it a true hidden gem. Located just 25 kilometers northwest of Ljubljana, this charming town is filled with cobblestone streets, ancient buildings, and the impressive Škofja Loka Castle. The castle offers panoramic views of the surrounding valley, and the town itself is perfect for a leisurely stroll to discover traditional Slovenian architecture. Škofja Loka is also home to the annual Škofja Loka Passion Play, which has been performed for centuries, making it an excellent destination for history and culture lovers.

- Velika Planina

For a truly unique experience, visit Velika Planina, a high-altitude plateau in the Kamnik-Savinja Alps. This stunning destination is known for its traditional wooden herder's huts, which remain in use by local shepherds during the summer months. The area is perfect for hiking, skiing, or simply enjoying the tranquility of the landscape. The Velika Planina cable car offers a scenic ride up to the plateau, where visitors can explore the pastoral beauty of Slovenia's rural traditions. It's a great place to escape the crowds and enjoy Slovenia's natural beauty.

- The Karst Region and Lipica

The Karst region is a fascinating area that features a unique landscape of rolling hills, limestone cliffs, and caves. This region is home to the famous Postojna Cave and Škocjan Caves, but there are many lesser-known caves and tunnels worth exploring as well. The town of Lipica, famous for the Lipizzaner horses, is also an emerging destination for those seeking a combination of culture and nature. Visitors can tour the Lipica Stud Farm and learn about the breeding of these iconic horses, while the surrounding landscape offers opportunities for hiking, cycling, and wine tasting.

- Lake Bohinj

While Lake Bled often steals the spotlight, Lake Bohinj offers a quieter and more peaceful alternative. Nestled in the heart of the Triglav National Park, Bohinj is a stunning glacial lake surrounded by towering mountains and lush forests. It's an ideal spot for hiking, swimming, kayaking, and cycling. The nearby Vogel Ski

Resort provides winter sports opportunities, while the charming town of Bohinjska Bistrica offers a glimpse into traditional Slovenian life. The Savica Waterfall, one of Slovenia's most famous waterfalls, is also located near the lake and is easily accessible via a short hike.

- The Brda Region

Slovenia's Brda region is often called the country's "Tuscany" due to its rolling hills, vineyards, and olive groves. This scenic area, located near the Italian border, is a haven for food and wine lovers. The region is known for its high-quality wines, especially white wines like Rebula and Sauvignon Blanc, and its rich culinary heritage. The picturesque town of Dobrovo is the heart of the region, and visitors can tour the local wineries, dine at farm-to-table restaurants, and enjoy the tranquil countryside. The region is also home to the beautiful Grad Dobrovo, a Renaissance-style castle offering panoramic views of the vineyards and hills.

- Kozjak Waterfall

Tucked away in the remote hills of the Kobarid region, the Kozjak Waterfall is a stunning hidden gem that's often overlooked by tourists. This impressive waterfall cascades into a turquoise pool and is surrounded by lush green forest. A relatively easy hike leads to the waterfall, making it an accessible and peaceful spot for nature lovers. It's one of Slovenia's most beautiful and serene natural wonders, offering a perfect place to escape the crowds.

- The Idrija Mercury Mine

A UNESCO World Heritage site, the Idrija Mercury Mine offers a fascinating glimpse into Slovenia's industrial past. Located in the town of Idrija, this former mercury mine was once one of the largest and most important in Europe. Visitors can tour the underground tunnels, learn about the history of mercury mining, and explore the charming town that grew up around the mine. The town is also home to traditional lace-making crafts, and the Idrija Lace Centre is a great place to learn about this UNESCO-recognized craft.

- Rogla and Pohorje

For those seeking a quieter, less commercialized alternative to Slovenia's more famous ski resorts, the Rogla and Pohorje mountains in northeastern Slovenia offer a more relaxed atmosphere. The Rogla Ski Resort is ideal for skiing, snowboarding, and winter sports, while the surrounding Pohorje Hills provide excellent hiking and mountain biking trails in the warmer months. The region is known for its natural beauty, and visitors can enjoy peaceful walks through forests, across meadows, and along mountain lakes.

- Ptuj

Although Ptuj is one of Slovenia's oldest towns, it remains a hidden gem for many visitors. Located on the banks of the Drava River, Ptuj is known for its medieval castle, the charming Old

Town, and the annual Kurentovanje Carnival, one of Slovenia's most important cultural events. The town is also home to some excellent local wines, which visitors can sample at local vineyards and wine cellars. Ptuj is a great destination for those interested in history, culture, and authentic Slovenian experiences.

- Trenta Valley

Located in the heart of the Triglav National Park, the Trenta Valley is one of Slovenia's most stunning and secluded locations. Surrounded by towering peaks, the valley is perfect for hiking, cycling, and nature walks. The Soča River runs through the valley, offering opportunities for kayaking, rafting, and fishing. Trenta is also home to the Trenta Museum, where visitors can learn about the natural history and cultural heritage of the area. It's an ideal spot for anyone looking to explore Slovenia's wild and untamed landscapes.

Slovenia is filled with hidden gems and emerging destinations that offer a rich, authentic experience of the country's natural beauty and cultural heritage. These off-the-beaten-path locations provide an opportunity to escape the crowds and experience the true essence of Slovenia. Whether you're exploring tranquil lakes, ancient towns, or remote valleys, Slovenia's lesser-known treasures promise unforgettable experiences.

ACKNOWLEGDEMENT

ABOUT THE AUTHOR

Aria Wild is a passionate traveler, writer, and storyteller dedicated to inspiring others to explore the world and immerse themselves in diverse cultures. With a background in journalism and a lifelong curiosity about different ways of life, Aria has made it her mission to uncover the stories that make each destination unique.

Her love for travel began at an early age, sparked by family road trips and later nurtured through solo adventures to far-flung corners of the globe. Over the years, she has journeyed through bustling cities, serene countryside, and remote islands, documenting her experiences through vivid narratives and compelling photography.

Aria specializes in creating practical yet immersive travel guides designed to help readers connect deeply with the places they visit. She blends firsthand knowledge with a flair for uncovering hidden gems, ensuring her work resonates with both seasoned globetrotters and first-time travelers.

In addition to writing, Aria advocates for sustainable and responsible tourism. She believes in the importance of supporting local communities, preserving cultural heritage, and protecting the natural environment, and her work often highlights ways travelers can make a positive impact.

When she's not traveling, Aria enjoys hiking, experimenting with recipes from around the world, and indulging in her love for literature and art. She finds inspiration in the connections she forges with people and places, and she brings this sense of wonder and discovery to her writing.
Through her travel guides and essays, Aria Wild invites readers to see the world not just as tourists but as explorers with an open heart and mind, ready to embrace the beauty and complexity of the global tapestry.

SAFE TRAVEL

Made in the USA
Monee, IL
22 January 2025